Urban Renaissance:

A strategy for Neighbourhood Renewal and the Welfare Society

by

Dr Dick Atkinson

BREWIN
BOOKS

in
association
with

RESIDENTS FOR REGENERATION

First published by Brewin Books Ltd.
Studley, Warwickshire B80 7LG, April 2000.

■ In association with St Paul's Community Education Project Ltd., and the Balsall Heath Forum Ltd., The Tree Nursery, 82-89 St Paul's Road, Balsall Heath B12. Tel: 0121 446 6183.   Fax: 0121 440 5060.

■ Copies of Urban Renaissance can be obtained from the above address.

ISBN:
1 85858 165 6

Printed in Great Britain
by Warwick Printing Company Limited,
Theatre Street, Warwick, Warwickshire CV34 4DR.

RESIDENTS FOR REGENERATION

For Gill, Sophie and Jane.

"Civilisation hangs suspended, from generation to generation, by the gossamer strand of memory. If only one cohort of mothers and fathers fails to convey to its children what it has learned from its parents, then the great chain of learning and wisdom snaps. If the guardians of human knowledge stumble only one time, in their fall collapses the whole edifice of knowledge and understanding.

Jacob Neusner

"It takes a whole village to educate a child"

African saying

"Give a hungry man a fish and you make him dependent on you. Teach him how to fish and to make a fishing tackle and you make him independent."

Polish Saying.

"In order to see into the future we need to look far into the past."

Winston Churchill

Index

Preface

I left the world of academic sociology nearly thirty years ago to live and work in down town Birmingham. During this time I have had a number of unexpected and astonishing experiences denied to politicians. So has my friend Bob Holman who gave up a glittering career as Professor of Social Administration to become a professional 'good neighbour' in Glasgow's difficult Easterhouse estate. Over the years since leaving Academia, he and I have met a range of people who, like ourselves, have tried to rescue their inner and outer city areas from despair and have slowly formed local associations which enabled residents to aspire to a better tomorrow for themselves and their children.

None of us found our work to be easy or straight forward. We quickly discovered that there were no politically appropriate maps to chart our way forward. No political party held many or even some of the questions, let alone the answers. There was not even a language with which to articulate our findings. Indeed, whichever party was in power in central or local government seemed wedded to theories and policies which got in the way of understanding and made matters worse not better.

So, working with local people to kindle hope in place of despair was, for many years, achieved despite rather than because of the political 'system' and established ways of thinking. Yet, it must also be said, some of the progress we made was only achieved because good people in positions of political influence recognised what we were doing and, at some political risk to themselves, found ways of backing it. These practical and concerned people were, we discovered, to be found in each and every party. Indeed, it was as if they had inadvertently formed a kind of third, or is it fourth, party, an invisible and nameless one in conventional terms, but one which practitioners learned to identify as the home of the can-doers who cared and helped regardless of their particular party and its theories.

So, how can our excluded urban neighbourhoods be included and what has to change before an Urban Renaissance can take place? Just what is it about the theory and the practices of political parties which has made the task of rebuilding shattered communities so difficult? Why is it that as the parties stand they find it hard to accept the implications of what we and some of their own kind do? How must they change if they are to pull with us? Is the 'third way' suited to just one political party or the government? Or, does it represent an approach to social relations which is above and beyond politics and, as such, open to any and every party to benefit from? This book tries to answer these questions.

The ideas and suggestions contained in the book have been influenced by very many people. An earlier draft was read by Peter Lilley (Conservative), David Blunkett (Labour) and Ralf Dahrendorf (Lib-Dem). Each in turn gave a 'Welfare Society' lecture sponsored by DEMOS and NatWest. Other people include:

Professor Bob Holman, Sir Richard Knowles, Ian Edwards, Raja Amin, Gloria Dillion, Geoff Mulgan, Rev. Andrew Mawson, Dr. Stephen Thake, Paddy Ashdown, David Wilkinson, Dr. Jonathan Sacks, Dennis Minnis, Jim Amos, Jon Bright, Frank Field, Mick Rice, Bryan Stoten, Margaret Harrison, John Rennie, Anthony Coombs, Kathy Neugent, Abdul Hamid, Mark Riley, Phil Grainger, Peter Lambert, Sir Neville Simms, Tricia Zipfel, Charles Handy, David Hargreaves, Professor Anne Power, Marilyn Taylor, David Green, James Tooley, Alan Howarth, Simon Hubbard, Tom Bentley and many more people too numerous to mention. However, I am particularly grateful to Anita Halliday, Chris Wadhams and Ian Christie for their constructive criticism of earlier drafts. The best ideas are theirs. The errors which remain are mine.

I am most grateful to Sophie Atkinson, Nabila Shanaz, Lisa McMahon, Claire Shakespeare and Wamith Mockbill who have struggled to improve the words by typing and retyping them on more occasions than they care to recall.

Executive Summary

Good people of influence and power are becoming aware of the harshness of the reality of life for 30% of the population who cluster in the nation's 3,000 troubled inner and outer city urban areas. Hope flickers but it is dim and easily extinguished. The question is: "How to kindle it and enable it to burn brightly?" New solutions are needed, for old ones have failed.

Although large sums of taxpayers money (at least £100,000,000 per neighbourhood of 15,000 people) are poured into these areas every single year too much vanishes without trace and it can harm as well as help. It is, thus, largely wasted. The taxpayer knows this and is annoyed. The recipient knows it and is resentful. The give and take of this relationship is so impersonal it does not exist.

A variety of top-down attempts at regeneration have been tried over the last 40 years which, in effect, have poured billions of pounds worth of good money after bad and made little difference. They have tried to ameliorate the symptoms, but have not tackled the causes. The problem has thus grown more acute, not less. Government has now acknowledged this. No. 10 has a Social Exclusion Unit (SEU) whose brief is to include the excluded. It acknowledges that most people who live in these areas are not feckless. They do know what they want – a better life for themselves and their children. But, they do not know how to achieve it and the taxpayer does not know how to give it to them in a way which helps and does not hinder.

The causes of this malaise are beginning to be understood. But few know how they interact and even fewer know how they can be tackled. The SEU, Lord Rogers URBAN Task Force and the Government's new National Strategy for Neighbourhood Renewal need help if they are to succeed.

The huge departmental silos of the welfare state were created in an era when the industrial towns and communities were thriving and growing. Today they are of little use to the post-industrial town or its atomised, despairing, inner and outer city neighbourhoods. They were simply not designed to create self-sustaining neighbourhoods in which hope can be realised.

So, in order to regenerate the inner and outer city areas and make the wider society inclusive and harmonious, the radical reform of the Welfare State is proposed. It is not just social security benefits and pensions which need to change, but education, housing, health and policing in order to end dependence, create independence, new forms of self-governing mutual associations and new partnerships between the public, private and community sectors.

Hitherto, central and local government have delivered one-size-fits all public services across great swathes of the urban landscape without regard to the particular needs of distinct social and geographical communities to shape their own agenda and manage their own affairs. Existing best practice in the field, not political theory or ideology, shows that regeneration and renaissance will not take place unless enough of those who live in each area own the process of recovery and have resources and assets which give them real teeth. If this is to happen, each shattered inner and outer city neighbourhood needs:

- An identity which gives local pride and boundaries which are respected by town planners who previously delivered services throughout the whole territory covered by their urban authority without regard to many distinct geographical neighbourhoods which it contains.

- At least one Community Development Enterprise or Trust.

- A Neighbourhood Forum much as rural areas have a Parish Council which gives a voice to voiceless people.

- A Social Entrepreneur or Capacity Builder who can magic social capital from few resources, show people how to turn hope into reality and use their voices to realise that hope.

- The space and time needed to build mutual associations and an array of local people who have found the confidence to shape their life chances.

- The resources – buildings, staff and other assets required by those people before they can play their part.

- A Neighbourhood Development Plan to be costed, funded, implemented and reviewed year on year to achieve agreed outputs and targets.

- A new kind of public self-governing agency – the neighbourhood school, housing estate, local police force and health centre, which have both their own special task and the inter-agency one of neighbourhood regeneration.

- Civic Entrepreneurs who are the public counterpart of the Capacity Builder and who will run these self-governing agencies.

- A lead Civic Entrepreneur, to act as the Senior Manager of each troubled neighbourhood. Their proposed task is to staff the neighbourhood's devolved mini-town-hall, with a multidisciplinary task force of officers who are seconded from the Town Centre. These officers will help to implement the Neighbourhood Plan and liaise closely with the Forum and its team.

- In essence, it is proposed that the old, failed, way of managing the care of people and delivering services throughout each Local Authority's whole territory in urban areas is closed down and socially and geographically defined neighbourhoods of 2,000 to 20,000 people are reopened under new management with control over their own budgets.

- These proposals entail the radical reform of local government and the addition of participatory democracy to the representative kind.

- For the best part of 100 years the axiom which has guided social reforms is the redistribution of wealth and power from those who have to those who have not. This has not worked. Those at the cutting edge of development are telling us that in future the axiom to apply is that wealth and power and hope are latent in even the most deprived areas. Building the capacity of local people to the point where they can help themselves and develop their own forms of wealth and power is the hard new path to follow.

- There are many practical examples of success in different parts of the country which hold out hope for the future. It is proposed that these come together to start a rolling programme of reform which results in the Welfare State being replaced by the Welfare Society.

- This and future Governments are, therefore, asked to resource these proposals by helping the structure and organisation of local government and statutory agencies to change radically.

- Capacity Builders and Neighbourhood Managers are new professionals who will need their own special recruitment, training and support systems. They will be asking residents, professionals and councillors to act differently so, they too, will need support and training.

- A series of resident-led Regional Centres for Regeneration to complement a National Centre for Urban Renewal is called for. These centres will put resident led initiatives as well as these new professionals on the map and will collect and disseminate good practice.

- To include the previously excluded 3,000 neighbourhoods is an ambitious task. A rolling programme is called for which starts with successful pilots and takes in, say, 200 more each year for 15 years. Residents will only keep pace with such developments if, in addition to the National Centre, there are initially at least 4 regional ones which are led by experienced residents who can guide and support others in their region.

- There are national Inspectorates of schools, prisons and Social Services Departments. There should be an Inspectorate of Neighbourhoods, an Ofhood, with the powers and means to inspect all 3,000 troubled and at risk neighbourhoods within 4 years and to recommend further changes in management in these areas which are not taking the steps needed to recover.

- A culture change is called for. Governments alone can only resource and enable. If the troubled and excluded urban hinterland of our society is to become resilient and part of society, then the faith establishments, schools and many ordinary people in all walks of life must play a decisive part over a long period of time.

- The 'third way' is not a party political programme or a new '-ism'. Neither is it simply steering a path between the extremes and the left and the right. It is a broad based popular movement designed to mend the hole in the social ozone layer and, as such, is a social equivalent to the popular movement to steward our physical environment. It aims to include a third force of active citizens in the management of their own neighbourhoods. It is this powerful 3-way alliance of citizens, an enabling public state and the regulated private market that defines the real substance of the third way.

- Expecting people to behave responsibly, to care for themselves and each other and to exercise a greater control over the quality of life in urban areas implies the need for values, and a clear and distinct morality. If responsibilities are to be asserted as well as rights, then the post enlightenment laissez- fair culture of 'anything goes' must be questioned and placed within the context of a shared set of universal values.

- It is not just that good policies are called for, the culture change requires good people.

- The time is ripe. It is important to celebrate the early years of the new millennium not just with grand physical structures, domes and ferris wheels, but with vibrant, self-sustaining, social structures with which all can identify. As it has taken many years for the social and moral fabric of our inner and outer city neighbourhoods to unravel, it will take several decades to stitch it back together and create a new urban renaissance.

Chapter 1:

Introduction

As the new millennium becomes established, life is a privilege and exciting for many people in our society. They feel included in the mainstream of global events and capable of shaping the future. But theirs is not the only story to be told. There is another tale which tarnishes the glamour and reveals a malaise at the core of an otherwise happy story.

Throughout the twentieth century national leaders have worked to build an inclusive and harmonious society which looks after the weak as well as the strong. The outcome, however, has been the very opposite for 20% of the population who live in 2,000 troubled inner and outer city neighbourhoods while a further 10% teeter on the brink. Most people within this significant minority of 30% who live in 3,000 neighbourhoods know what they want. Their aspirations for themselves and, particularly, their children are clear – a fulfilling life enthused with hope. But, they lack confidence and there are too few local associations or support structures to enable them to realise their potential. So, they feel trapped by circumstances beyond their control. They feel excluded. They live in outer and inner city areas in which despair diminishes hope.

This is not just a misfortune for this minority. The majority is also adversely affected. The state now claims taxes from them to provide services for all, not just the 30%. Yet, the outcome is the very opposite of the intention. Hard-earned money is wasted and discord is created. Neither the giver nor receiver is happy. On the one hand, the taxpayer finds it hard to see their money used by the state to such little effect. On the other hand, those on the receiving end resent having to live in neighbourhoods which are stalked by despair. As a result, society is not at ease with itself. It is not well managed or as economically and socially productive as it could be. It does not 'flow'. It grates.

This is surprising. For over 100 years the political parties and the departments of state which they manage have striven to eliminate want, disease, ignorance and despair. While policy makers are now beginning to understand why previous attempts at inclusion have failed, the policy levers which they can pull have not in the past resulted in real assistance on the ground. Can they be helped to make the levers work this time? In particular can those on the ground respond to those levers and form new top-down/bottom-up partnerships which work?

1) The nature of Local Government.

Each Local Authority, its Education, Housing, the Environment and Planning Departments as well as the Police and Health Authorities grew up when the Industrial Revolution was in full swing and new, vibrant, self-sustaining urban neighbourhoods were arising. These departments and authorities developed specialist, vertically organised bureaucracies which delivered a variety of services for people throughout the whole of their authority area regardless of the many individually distinct neighbourhoods of which it was comprised.

Today, the Industrial Revolution which these departments and authorities serviced is over, but urban life has yet to find a new purpose. The Industrial economy and the communities it sustained have collapsed, particularly in inner and outer city areas. Today, 30% of the population suffer from not just one form of deprivation. They have to withstand joined-up problems. The once effective specialist structures of local government, the Police and Health Authority are simply not equipped to provide the joined-up solutions which are called for. In their place a new horizontal, inter-departmental, neighbourhood specific approach is required to meet the quite new post-industrial need for urban regeneration.

2) The importance of Whitehall and Town Hall

A grand illusion has ill-served the quality of urban life for too long. It has been supposed that the pinnacle of politics and public life is to be found in Whitehall and the Cabinet. But the great decisions of the day do not depend on this or that national political party, or on their grip on national government. For, the vital questions which most concern people include:

★ How can the litter be moved from the gutter outside my home?

★ How can I know that my children can play safely in the street and local park and that I can walk out alone without fear?

★ How can my local school help my child to do their best?

★ How can I be sure that I will have a job and retain it?

★ How can I feel proud of the neighbourhood I live in?

★ How can I both give and receive in mutual association with others and feel fulfilled as a member of a community?

★ How can I find hope and realise my ambitions?

While these questions can only be answered at a very practical and local level, they need to be resourced by local and central government. And, to do this, we must not only rethink the way that politics and local government are conceived, we must also redefine the role that ordinary people can play in determining the quality of their lives. We must now add everyday participatory democracy to the representative kind from which ordinary people shy away in increasing numbers when elections are held once a year or every five years.

3) From Welfare State to Welfare Society.

Beveridge's Welfare State marked a vital stage in the creation of a caring society. Since his day, for decade after decade successive governments of all political persuasions have built upon the foundations he laid. As time went on, however, the state came to encompass not just individual benefits to the most needy but also the provision of education, housing, health and safety to most people. By gaining the public ownership of key industries it even intruded into the way we ordered our economic affairs. Indeed, like the over protective parent who couldn't allow his child to leave the nest, it came to provide too much and, in so doing, made many people dependent upon its one-size-fits-all monopolistic services which compared unfavourably with those which the most affluent could choose and buy from a variety of independent suppliers. The unintended outcome has been the diminution of people's sense of self-reliance, enterprise and communal responsibility. The caring state inadvertently became an obstacle to social, educational and cultural as well as to economic progress.

We now know from practical experience that personal welfare can be delivered just as readily if not better by little local social associations and enterprises as well as the family and home. Because they are so close to where people live, they can identify with, influence and improve upon them. If we forget this, allow them to wither and, in effect, take more out of society than we put back in then we create a hole in the social ozone layer which, we are just beginning to understand, is as dangerous to life as the hole in the physical ozone layer. The realisation is now dawning that we must steward the social environment in which we live just as surely as we must steward the physical environment. So, 50 years on from Beveridge, the burning questions of our time have become: "How can we move from the industrial attitudes, remote institutions and funding mechanisms of the Welfare State to the more personal and mutual ones of the Welfare Society?" How can we create an urban renaissance which affects not just our inner and outer urban areas but the whole of our society?

Chapter one
    Paints the scene and suggests the need to move from a Welfare State to a Welfare Society in order to investigate the way we care for each other.

Chapter two
    Looks at a typical outer city area and sees how a head teacher and taxpayer both despair at its lack of social cohesion.

Chapter three

Considers the causes of the problems facing inner and outer city areas and identifies the way the Welfare State is organised as a key culprit.

Chapter four

Examines why governments are already unpacking the way they have managed the nation's economic and social assets and looks beyond state delivered services to ones sustained in small neighbourhoods.

Chapter five

Shows that ordinary people, social and civic entrepreneurs have already made much practical progress. They provide models which illustrate the way forward.

Chapter six

Describes the different ingredients involved in neighbourhood management and outlines what the local authority of the future will look like.

Chapter seven

Points out that a new form of participatory democracy must be added to the purely representative kind both to make self-governing local agencies in small neighbourhoods accountable and to breath fresh credibility into representative democracy.

Chapter eight

Describes the huge rolling programme of national and local reform which is just beginning and the mechanisms which must drive it forward including resident led centres for regeneration and an Inspectorate of Neighbourhoods.

Chapter nine

Shows that common values are needed to give point and purpose to the emerging Welfare Society and to motivate good people who are as important as good policies.

Chapter ten

Concludes by showing how the first and second political ways can be distilled into a third more socially resonant one fit for the early decades of the new Millennium and the renaissance for which we yearn.

These chapters reveal a challenging and difficult story which tells us that the excluded can't be included simply by redistributing money to them, giving them extra funds or by special regeneration initiatives like Inner City Partnership, NDC or the Single Regeneration Budget. Rather, long established ways of thinking about, valuing and organising society must change. What is called for will take time and needs the support not just of this but of many governments and the pioneering illustration of practical examples which show the way for others to follow. In other words, the situation we describe is so serious and it is so important that a sustained national campaign is required. Nothing less will suffice if we are to enable people trapped within the 3,000 troubled neighbourhoods to realise their dreams and become part of the mainstream of life.

The twentieth century began with a flourishing of the sense of civic duty and the construction of a great range of public works from sewers to Town Halls. However, as times passed, as happens to almost every physical and social innovation, these once new structures failed to adapt to new circumstances. Like the docks and mines of the industrial era, these social and political structures came to inhibit social development. It is, therefore, appropriate that the first decades of the new Millennium begin with an urban renaissance, with the construction of new forms of social and political management which are appropriate to a new age, which include the excluded, re-connect those who give with those who receive and make the wider society more enterprising, productive and morally clear headed.

Chapter 2:

A head teacher, excluded neighbourhoods and a taxpayer

In 1990 a head teacher described to the author the municipally designed and managed outer-ring catchment area of his school. He said, "It is an a-cultural social desert. There are, no local associations and many parents are on their own. They have no partner, no relatives nearby and are at their wits' end. Their children are often out of control and they can find no other adult to offer guidance about how to cope."

"My entire school", he said, "turns over every three years." He explained: "One third of my pupil's parents move every year – to live with another partner, in search of a job or because they have been evicted for rent arrears. Thus, every three years I have an entirely new school population." The same, of course, was true of his catchment community. "There is no consistency," he said. "There is no chance of developing any kind of school or communal tradition which might bring stability and respect. No wonder my children are lost and don't know how to behave. They have no moral yardstick by which to measure right or wrong and which might tell them how to behave."

It is as if Jonathan Sacks' had been listening. For, in his eloquent book, 'The Politics of Hope', he wrote that: "Tradition is to morality what memory is to personality, and when we lose it we become prey to a kind of collective Alzheimer's Disease."

How many such inner and outer-city areas are there in this land? How many are moving in that direction or manage to retain just enough resilience to withstand the more extreme manifestations of it?

Using the Acorn classification, the Social Exclusion Unit's third publication, Bringing Britain Together, estimated that the answer is between 1,600 and 4,000 neighbourhoods. Other researchers identified 1,370 estates. The English House Condition Survey calculated there were 3,000 such places. If an average of 5,000 people live in each of these 3,000 neighbourhoods, then a total of 15,000,000 people live in them. This figure coincides with the author's calculation that 20% of our neighbourhoods suffer in the way the head teacher described while a further 10% are at risk, – 30% in all.

Distressed by the head teacher's account, the author took a decent and reasonably affluent businessman to the school and its catchment estate in the hope that he would see the point of helping in some way. He got very cross and asked why he should 'Throw good money after bad'. He explained: "My business pays tens of thousands of pounds a year in taxes and I pay my own fair whack to the politicians. And, with it, they create this? Then you come along and ask me to pick up the pieces ... Look, if I ran my business like they organise this place my shareholders would have thrown me out years ago – or I'd have gone bust. So, tell me, what's the point?"

A policy adviser who accompanied us accused the business man of seeing the people of the estate as feckless and unwilling to help themselves. He exploded, "Don't try that one," he said. "I'm not blaming the people who live here. It's the people who manage the place and the politicians. Don't accuse me of not caring. I could weep seeing this, but over 300 people are in work because of me, because I manufacture and sell a product (car components) which people want to buy. There's nothing I can do with this. Come back when you can tell me you have sacked the managers and changed the politicians. Until then, don't waste my time and I certainly won't waste my money."

Just as we must ask how many neighbourhoods like this there are, so we must also ask how many people there are like this business man who work hard and care but feel that the fruits of their labour and energies are squandered by the prevailing system? How much could and would they do if only there was a fresh, productive, relationship between the private, the public and the third sector of the community? How can we persuade people in the neighbourhood, business people and politicians that they can develop a relationship which works to their mutual understanding and satisfaction – which builds hope in the whole of society? How can we create a society which does not grate, but which flows in productive harmony?

The nature of the problem

First of all, it is important to accept the nature and scale of the problem. Indeed, in the areas we describe there is not just one problem, but many. These can be summarised as follows:

- The once extended family has in many cases shrunk beyond the two to the single parent family. The support of the extended family and its accumulated knowledge about child-raising is no longer available to the parent of today.

- Health is generally poor. More children die in infancy than elsewhere. Life expectancy is up to 10 years shorter in the areas we describe than in their affluent counterparts.

- The proportion of home ownership is low. More houses are managed either by housing associations or local authorities.

- The pavements and parks are ill-maintained. The green environment is litter strewn and the built environment is daubed with graffiti.

- Educational attainment is low. Ofsted tells us that 30% of schools are poor. Most of these are to be found serving the 30% of the population who live in inner and outer city neighbourhoods.

- There are few leisure amenities or local associations.

- There are few if any local resources or assets such as buildings or land which people or local associations own.

- The level of unemployment is high. It can be as much as 50%. More women than men are in work.

- The level of crime and the fear of crime are both disproportionately high.

- Those with zest and ambition first send their children to schools elsewhere then, if they have the means to do so, they move home. There is, thus, a net exodus of talent and role models. Only those who cannot afford to live else where stay.

- The professionals who staff the statutory agencies which provide services – city departments, police, health – are usually well meaning. But they tend not to stay long either. For, they see such neighbourhoods as stepping stones to a more rewarding career move elsewhere.

These problems were well summarised in the Social Exclusion Unit's report, Bringing Britain Together, which compared the rest of England with 44 deprived districts. Compared with other places, in these 44 districts there was:

- "Nearly two thirds more **unemployment**.

- Almost one and a half times the proportion of **lone parent house-holds**

- One and a half times the **underage pregnancy rate**.

- Almost a third of **children growing up in families on Income Support** (against less than a quarter in the rest of England).

- 37 per cent of 16 year olds without **a single GCSE at grades A-C,** against 30 per cent for the rest of England.

- more than twice as many nursery/primary and more than five times as many secondary **schools on special measures**.

- roughly a quarter more adults with **poor literacy or numeracy**.

- **mortality ratios** 30 per cent higher, adjusting for age and sex.

- levels of **vacant housing** one and a half times elsewhere.

- two to three times the levels of **poor housing, vandalism and dereliction.**

- more young people, with **child densities** a fifth higher.

- nearly four times the proportion of **ethnic minority** residents."

In an astonishingly perceptive in depth study, Dark Heart, Nick Davies reports that too many people who live in troubled neighbourhoods have come to feel "there to be no point to life, no point to families, no point to neighbours, no point to going to school... ...life is queuing for a giro, propping up a wall on the corner of a street, sleeping till the afternoon and watching telly till dawn... ...it is being pregnant for no reason, being jobless with no hope. It means nothing, it has fallen apart."

In a series of detailed reports, Nick explores life in the inner area of Nottingham and a dozen other parts of the country. He describes just how difficult life is for many, many, people. "And it is there – in the hollow inside them, in their indifference to everyone, including themselves, in their total acceptance of pain, in their contempt for law and all the rest of their surroundings – it is there that the children ... of Nottingham show their common origin, in these thousands of battered ... (neighbourhoods) which together form the heartland of the undeserved country of the poor."

Another head teacher remembered the time the archbishop of Canterbury visited her school and listened to the children sing. He asked her "about the children's eyes – why was it that the youngest had a sparkle.... while the ten and eleven year olds looked so dull and lifeless? And so she told him the truth. "These children have no hope" she said. "They live in a state of despair."

Together, all these disadvantages add up to the joined – up problems which government ministers, No. 10's Social Exclusion Unit and the National Strategy for Renewal now recognise. That is, they do not appear here and there, scattered about the population at random. They are piled one on top of the other. Those who live in the neighbourhoods we are concerned with suffer from and are weighed down by most, if not all of them.

Special aid might be able to tackle one or other of these problems. But if the rest are left alone, they will quickly combine to defeat that aid. It may be difficult and daunting, but common sense suggests that all must be tackled at once if the people who suffer from them are not to be sucked down by them, but are to leap free and establish a fuller, rewarding life.

Perhaps we can muster the will to accomplish this task and create Communities of Hope from Neighbourhoods of Despair if we understand how these multiple problems have arisen and the nature of the one problem, as yet not specified, which acts like glue to bind them all together – the lack of confidence and spirit, the belief that these life circumstances can't be changed for the better. People who live in troubled neighbourhoods know very well what they want for themselves and their children. But they do not have the confidence, skills or vision to make things work for them or to realise their dreams.

Chapter 3:

The Causes of The Problem

There is no one cause of the problems which blight so many neighbourhoods. Demographic factors are one significant influence. So is the gathering pace of technological change and the globalisation of markets. But one major additional cause has recently been recognised which has troubled consciences and accepted political truths. It is the Welfare State itself, the way we manage care for each other and the provision of caring services.

William Beveridge intended social security benefits and pensions to support the working man and his family through brief times of sickness and retirement. However, today some people are now unemployed for very long periods and most now live for 20 and 30 years into retirement. The costs of providing so much support for so many people have risen astronomically. Since the Second World War costs have risen from 1% to 13% of GDP, that is, to £95 billion per year. Far more people than ever before are dependent on these state payments. As Frank Field has documented to almost everyone's acceptance, the result is that:

> "Hard work is penalised by the loss of entitlement. Incentives reinforce welfare dependence. Honesty is punished by a loss of income. It is in this sense that welfare is the enemy within. Its rules actively undermine the moral fabric of our characters. In so doing it eats into the public domain and so helps erode the wider moral order of society."

Too many people have therefore become dependent on state benefits. They do not see any possibility of getting a job and earning their own money. Their income is derived from taxes paid by others whom they can't see or identify with. Because the state is so large and remote it is seen as impersonal. While a few still will not claim their entitlement out of pride, most do so and some will 'cheat the system' if they can.

(a) Health, Housing, Education, the Environment and Crime.

This is not all. There is far more to the Welfare State than benefits and pensions. Since before the beginning of this Century, caring social reformers also wanted people to have decent housing, a school their children could attend, a National Health Service and a police force – all provided for people by the state and paid for by taxes, hence, free at the point of delivery. The sense of fervour built up as the first half of the 20th Century unfolded. It culminated in the reforms made during the Second World War by the coalition Government and by the 1945 Labour Government led by Clement Attlee.

The Conservative Secretary of State for Education, Rab Butler, put in place the 1944 Education Act. It extended state education for all so that everyone could go to school from 5 to 15 years of age. Aneurin Bevan took just a little longer before devising and putting in place the National Health Service in 1948.

A succession of Labour and Conservative Ministers knocked down the old 'slums' and the huge council estates of the 1950's and 1960's were created. Home Secretary after Home Secretary spent more and more on the police force whose numbers grew apace.

Thus, after the war, the Welfare State took not so much a step forward as a quantum leap as it advanced on all social fronts. It came to encompass:

– The provision of Social Security Benefits including pensions.

– The provision of houses

– The provision of education

– The provision of medical care

– The provision of safety and order

(b) The Private Sector – the Economy

With the benefit of hindsight, the observer might suppose that the state had expanded far enough by intruding into so many personal, social and educational walks of life. Yet, its ambitions also extended to encompass economic activity. Since the days of Joseph Chamberlain in Birmingham most people had long supposed that 'civic duty' was the best way of building sewers and providing the public utilities of water, gas and electricity. It seemed only a simple logical extension to include the great industries of coal, iron and steel, shipbuilding and the railways. Thus, for almost the whole of the twentieth century, Clause 4 of the Labour Party's constitution committed it to nationalising the 'commanding heights' of the economy as well as providing welfare services covering most aspects of individual, family and communal life.

Indeed, between 1945 and 1978 it seemed that this objective might be realised and that for a civil servant or policy maker to think otherwise was eccentric. Certainly, the post-Attlee Conservative governments of Eden, Macmillan, Home and Heath made no attempt to de-nationalise the large swathes of the economy which had passed into the collective hands of the state and which Harold Macmillan once eloquently and movingly defined as the nation's "family silver".

All governments merely tried to work the same consensual system better than their opponents could. In such circumstances, not surprisingly, the bureaucracies of central and local government grew and grew while the frown on the taxpayer's forehead deepened and despair in those neighbourhoods which concern us took root and multiplied.

(c) Funding the Welfare State

Once, taxation was small. It was only used by the state to fund wars and internal security. Today it is large and also funds all the great domestic departments of state. People are no longer able to decide how to spend a significant portion of what they earn. The caring and 'enlightened' Government of the Welfare State spends it on their behalf in a determined and praiseworthy attempt to make social progress. Social Security benefits now cost the average family £80.00 per week. Add in all other costs and this sum rises to £240.00 per week. This is £12,480 per year. When defence costs are removed, the total spending by the state in Britain on domestic welfare is now £288,000,000,000 and rising (see figures 1 and 2).

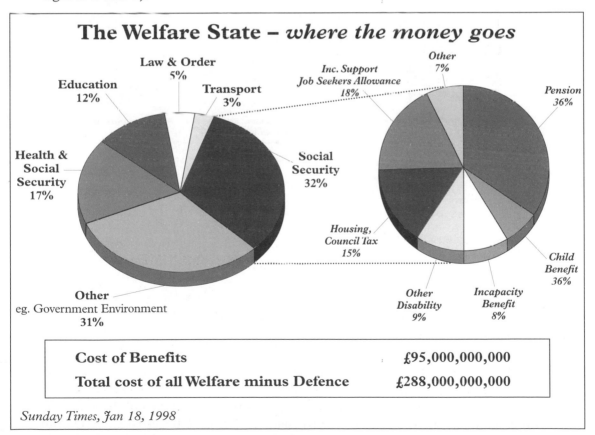

The Welfare State – *where the money goes*

Law & Order 5%
Education 12%
Transport 3%
Inc. Support Job Seekers Allowance 18%
Other 7%
Pension 36%
Health & Social Security 17%
Social Security 32%
Housing, Council Tax 15%
Child Benefit 36%
Other eg. Government Environment 31%
Other Disability 9%
Incapacity Benefit 8%

Cost of Benefits	**£95,000,000,000**
Total cost of all Welfare minus Defence	**£288,000,000,000**

Sunday Times, Jan 18, 1998

Figure 1

From this total spending by the State on Welfare it is possible to calculate how much of taxpayer's money is spent on the average neighbourhood of, say, 5,000 dwellings, or 15,000 residents. This total is £91,500,000. The figure is greater, of course, for the typical inner and outer city area. It could be as much as double the average – £183,000,000. Even supposing it is 'only' a little more, say, £100,000,000, this is an astonishing amount of taxpayer's money to spend on creating Neighbourhoods of Despair. What is even more surprising is that nobody knows what this figure actually is and that nobody is accountable for it. It is only now that the questions are being posed.

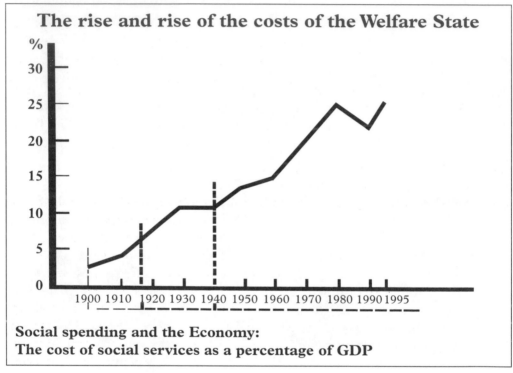

Figure 2

It follows that if, as has hitherto been the case, we spend yet more money in trying to help troubled neighbourhoods to improve when we do not know what is currently being spent on them or who, if anyone, is in charge then it too will be wasted. We are likely only to make the joined-up problems which people face worse. Rather, we need to calculate what we are spending, then spend it differently and effectively. However, before considering how to spend money differently, it is important to consider why we have spent so many years spending it in the way we have.

(d) Legitimising the Welfare State

The reasons for the growth, cost and scope of the post-war Welfare State, are various. They include:

1. Compassion. After the ravages of the industrial revolution it seemed sensible and caring to help people who were poor, sick and deprived of many of life's basic amenities by providing things for them.

2. Most bureaucracies develop a self-perpetuating momentum. Once created and set in motion they tend to find more and more things to do and to develop an empire. Success is measured in industrial terms of size and scope. Understandably, successive governments strove to spend ever more than their predecessors on all aspects of social life.

3. As important, perhaps more so, is the way we came to think society worked and how social change or progress could be engineered. For 200 years a set of assumptions and attitudes, a way of thinking, has been slowly evolving which tailored the way we set about creating a caring and progressive society. It is worth dwelling on this point for a moment. If we don't, we risk it obstructing our plea to spend money differently.

Copying the rise and rise of the natural sciences, the enlightened founding fathers of sociology supposed that if we looked beneath the variety of 'irrational' traditional social life we could also uncover basic rational social laws which determined people's conduct. It followed, they thought, that if we applied these laws to the government of society then enlightened administrators could produce a similar ever rising curve of social progress to match scientific progress. While this view denigrated the concepts of individuality, choice, variety and the notion that people behave in ways which are quite unlike atoms in the physical world, it seemed at first to be both true and to produce results.

Regardless of what people actually thought or believed, the new theory deduced that their action was formed by social circumstances. People did not shape events, they were shaped by them. So, if enlightened politicians and administrators intervened in society and changed the context in which people lived, it would change the people for the better. Thus, for example, if the State increased taxes and redistributed income by boosting benefits and creating institutions – houses, schools, hospitals, police – for all, then it should be possible to make progress and include all in the good life. Politicians were very excited. It seemed that if they redistributed wealth and the state created more and more caring institutions then poverty would be eliminated.

However, a major consequence of 200 years of social 'progress' since the Enlightenment has been that in all vital aspects of ordinary people's lives the balance has slowly shifted from traditional and morally driven 'bottom-up' self-reliant personal/private and neighbourly provision to 'top – down' dependent collective/public provision. What people had once created, sustained and paid for themselves, albeit often glaringly inadequately, gradually came to be provided for them by well meaning politicians of all parties. This provision was no longer delivered as personal family or neighbourly gifts or charity, such that the donor expected something in return and the recipient felt obligated to give it, but impersonally through enforced taxation and, thus, via the remote, ever growing, bureaucracies of state.

The changing balance from minor state and major private provision of housing, health, education and safety to major state and minor private provision was not scattered randomly through society. Like other social deprivations, it clustered dramatically in those areas which suffer other ills – the inner and outer areas of our towns and cities and impoverished rural areas. It has become the glue which binds the joined up problems together in these areas and all but creates the self-fulfilling prophecy that people are fashioned by the social situation they are in and can't influence or change it.

That is, multiple deprivation and joined-up problems feed one further and final concern. It is the most worrying and debilitating of all – the sense of exclusion and the fatalistic powerlessness to do anything to help oneself or to remedy the situation one is in. Most people in the areas we describe feel buffeted by circumstances beyond their control. The only choice open to them is to move, not to change or improve the situation where they live. And few can afford to move. So, those who stay behind can hardly afford to hope. They, like everyone, can dream but they feel these dreams are dimmed by the despair of everyday reality.

This major characteristic distinguishes troubled modern neighbourhoods from working class industrial pre - war places of material poverty. For, relatively speaking, the post-industrial areas are not materially poor. Certainly this is true if they are compared with their equivalent of the 1920's and 1930's, when the Welfare State was being conceived.

Today, although relatively speaking almost all are materially more affluent, a significant number of people in troubled neighbourhoods lack the capacity, spirit and will to do anything about the problems they face.

It is a peculiar irony, therefore, that although such people are materially better off than their counterparts of 100 years ago, they are, in this sense, spiritually poorer and powerless to help themselves.

So, it seems that while the Enlightenment has been with us for 200 years and the last 100 years have been spent in trying to help people out of material poverty we have done the very opposite and created for a significant minority in our society a new kind of social and cultural deprivation – an inability to help themselves and, thus, dependence – which is as, if not more, debilitating than economic poverty.

For most of this century, the shift from personal to impersonal, subjective to rational, moral to value-free, local to national and communal to public was thought to be good and the reason why the curve of social progress would rise sharply in the same way that the curve of scientific progress had done.

As it turns out, people do not fit the theories which ideologies sought to impose upon them. As Osborne and Gaebler have taught us: recent developments show that social laws and collective national plans could work only as long as the politicians and administrators who ran the top-down pyramid like bureaucracies of industrial society "had enough information to take reasonable decisions which those at the bottom of the pyramid could not query or improve upon; as long as most people worked with their hands and not their brains; as long as there were mass, undiscriminating markets; as long as most people had similar needs; as long as the Western industrial nations" had no serious competitors which could rival them.

Today, the hierarchical, bureaucratically ordered, world which the social administrator helped to legitimise is fading into the past. As Osbourne and Gaebler point out, in the hi-tech, post-industrial society "people get access to information almost as fast as their leaders do. We now live in a knowledge-based economy, in which educated workers bridle at commands and demand high quality and extensive choice." Today it would be no more acceptable for Henry Ford to say to his customers: "You can have a model T car in any colour you want provided it is black" than it is to say: "You can have any pair of spectacles, house or school you want provided it is the off-the-peg pair of national health specs, estate or school to which your child will be sent."

Osborne and Gaebler tell us that the top-down pyramid-like bureaucracies and institutions developed during the industrial era increasingly fail us in today's post-industrial society. Today's environment "demands institutions that deliver high quality goods and services.... It demands institutions that are responsive to their customers, offering choices of non-standardised services; that lead by persuasion and incentives rather than commands; that give their employees a sense of meaning and control, even ownership. It demands institutions that empower citizens rather than simply serving them."

Indeed, it demands a very different kind of society from the one which enlightened sociologists felt was inevitable and which, for a while, their theories made universal. And it requires a different view of how people who live in neighbourhoods of multiple deprivation can realise their hopes and ambitions.

Chapter 4:

Thinking the Unthinkable – Beyond the Welfare State

(a) The Private Sector

The advent of consumer choice and international competition first persuaded successive governments in the 1980s to give the private sector its head and release it from the protective grip of state ownership. The nationalised giants of coal, iron and ship building withered in the face of global competition and the new era of the silicone chip. They were simply costing too much for too little return. Even the Labour Party eventually bowed to the inevitable and replaced its constitutional intention to nationalise the commanding heights of the economy with one which talks about the family and the community.

(b) The Public Sector-Benefits

In the '80s and '90s the governments of all the developed countries also began to question the way the state funded pensions and employment, housing and child benefits. How could the spiralling cost and responsibility be shifted from the remote, collective, state to the individual and family? Only when Frank Field's vigorous analysis was added to that of Peter Lilley did more and more people in this country begin to think thoughts which for most of the century had been politically incorrect and unthinkable.

Until recently, we looked back at the large pre-war extended family of uncles and aunts, grand parents and a husband and wife as being 'Victorian', over-bearing and oppressive to the growing child. But, in shrinking from the extended family to the two and single parent one, the outcome for the child has not been liberty and choice. For many, the result has been license and an inability to shape and control their adult lives.

We all know how hard it is to care for children when only one or two voices and one or two pairs of hands are available. Most make an heroic attempt. But we now understand more fully how helpful grandparents and others were in the past. They not only passed on wise parenting skills which are now lost, they acted as baby minders allowing parents a much needed break etc. etc.. The state is no substitute. But it has tried to take on many of the functions including the income which the extended family once provided. At first, the Labour party denounced those Conservatives who questioned these developments as uncaring and "anti single parents". Now, we are all beginning to recognise that if we are really to help the two let alone the single parent family to care for the next cohort of children we must find more effective and personal forms of child support than the state can offer.

This politically and emotionally sensitive point is more easily understood in connection with unemployment benefits. We can now readily accept that it did not help an unemployed person to signal to them that they need not look for a job because they would be paid by the state to do nothing, if necessary, for most of their life. Welfare to Work schemes now provide training and job experience opportunities and only the long term sick and disabled need continuing support.

Similarly, pension reforms are beginning to suggest that new more effective ways of personally saving for old age may eventually supplement or replace the inadequate state pension. Indeed, an array of reforms are being considered which shift the emphasis from state benefits to personal responsibilities and the targeting of state support towards those who are in real need for as short a period as is reasonably possible. That is, we are returning to the principle which Beveridge originally expressed from a situation which had developed its own debilitating, all encompassing, logic.

Not everyone yet accepts the need for these reforms. Some, especially on the old Labour left, still champion people's rights and argue that encouraging people not to be dependent and to become self-reliant is somehow unjust and that the begrudging tax-payer is greedy and unkind. But the mood is changing.

Most people are coming to recognise that the greatest injustice is done by those who protest that poor people are best helped by doing things for them, and that the greatest service is done by those who push them towards self-reliance.

This principle has long been understood with regard to social and economic development in the under-developed Third World. Many years ago, Erich Schumacher wrote, in Small is Beautiful: "Give a man a fish, as the saying goes, and you help him a little bit for a very short while...(however)... the man's continuing livelihood will still be dependent upon you for replacements. But teach him to make his own fishing tackle and you have helped him to become not only self-supporting, but also self-reliant and independent.."

It makes caring sense to apply this matter of fact principle to those individual children, parents, unemployed people and pensioners who suffer in this developed country's underdeveloped inner and outer city areas. However, it will take many years and several governments before these reforms are all in place and the benefits of them are felt by all. In particular, family support and pension reforms will take a whole generation before the value of them reaches everyone. As governments normally like the quick fix and photo opportunity which boost their chances of winning the next election, it will take real courage and statesmanship to take the necessary long view.

Yet, while the sound and fury of the debate is now abating, it has distracted the mind from the fact that family support, unemployment, social security benefits and pensions are only relatively small aspects of the Welfare State.

Houses, Health and Schools

Social Security and Welfare benefits are not the only area of the Welfare state in which it is important to think the unthinkable. The ideas which people like Peter Lilley and Frank Field have pioneered in the realm of benefits and pensions have been picked up by others in the arenas of public housing, state schools, health and public safety.

Some people have bought their own Local Authority built and managed house. Housing Associations now manage an increasing number of houses and whole estates, once owned and managed by local authorities, are now controlled either by "not for profit" housing companies or the tenants themselves. Indeed, Birmingham is considering selling all its municipal houses to housing associations. Lambeth may 'give away' 40,000 of its homes.

The health funds which were once administered by local authorities have been opened up. Both Hospitals and groups of primary carers have their own cost centres and can manage their affairs more sensitively.

It may now seem strange that for 50 years no one knew until the late 80's and early 90's what each of the nation's 24,000 schools cost or what the outcome was of their pupils' 11 years of compulsory education. Each school's budget had become hopelessly entangled within the overall budget of their Local Education Authority (LEA). In this sense, neither the LEA nor each school knew what it cost or could tell whether the money it was spending was being used effectively or not.

The notion that, as with a private enterprise, each Head Teacher or Governor should be aware of what their particular school cost them, let alone hold that cost in their own bank and spend it as they saw fit to produce ever better results for their pupils was at first anathema to the collectivist and bureaucratic education establishment. Even worse, nobody supposed it was appropriate to ask what the results or outcomes of educational expenditure were. How did results compare year on year? How did they compare with other similar schools? At first, the very question was dismissed. Only today are those who run the education establishment beginning to accept the common sense of it. Yesterday we were supposed to ask: "How much more money can we put into education and how can we account for it by representative democratic means? Today, we realise we should be asking: "What outputs in terms of educational achievements are we getting and how do we hold teachers, governors and parents to account for poor results?"

(c) Neighbourhoods

However, everyone is still unclear about what the costs of welfare add up to in the places where people live, in particular in any one of the troubled neighbourhoods which are the principal subject of this book. How much money is put into them with the outcome that the joined up problems described earlier have steadily got worse? Is it the £100,000,000 which we conservatively estimated or is it the £183,000,000 which seems possible?

Either way, this is a huge sum with which to create the outputs which disgusted the author's visiting businessman and from which the resident would flee if given the option.

Nobody in local or central government whom the author has asked knows the cost. Anne Power has had one stab at it but left various items from the equation. At last people in the Treasury and The Social Exclusion Unit have also posed the question and are working on the answer.

It is difficult to overstate how important it is to get the answer. For, once it is known, then it will be possible to ask such elementary questions as: Is it worth it? Are there more productive ways of spending it? What proportion of it can be disassembled and reassembled in different ways? Even, shock and horror, can fresh management use less of it to better effect?

Why have we supposed that it is not necessary to manage or quantify the taxpayer's and state's input into inner and outer city neighbourhoods at all? The question needs to be underlined. For, on reflection, it is surely quite astonishing that failing neighbourhoods have never had a budget or a structure of management, or a person who is responsible for that management. The sums of money we describe and the failing services they fund are all separately delivered by separate agencies via separate bureaucracies and none are targeted at socially defined geographical areas of the kind we describe and in which real people live. At least schools knew where their boundaries were and had a head teacher even though he/she did not know until recently what his/her school cost.

It is heartening to acknowledge that the government now accepts that joined up problems can only be tackled by joined up solutions and that an overarching solution is likely to be holistic budgeting and neighbourhood management.

Meanwhile, until we do know what the answers are, there seams to be little point in giving Local Authorities additional money to put right the wrong created by the far greater sums of money which are already being spent on their neighbourhoods. Doing so would risk making the taxpayer as angry as the author made his business friend when he asked him to help just one such estate. Yet, whisper it softly, since the 1960's many many billions of taxpayer's pounds have been thrown by the welfare State at troubled areas on top of the costly mainstream budgets described. Little wonder it is difficult to point to any area which has been successfully regenerated by this means.

(d) Previous attempts at urban aid

Even before the various Welfare reforms described above got underway, governments had known for 30 years that the end of the industrial revolution posed serious problems for inner and outer city urban areas and that, if nothing else, the municipal housing estates which replaced working class terraced houses had merely created more problems. Many caring and sophisticated people devised and tried to implement a succession of 'urban renewal' initiatives to alleviate the new kind of urban problem. Yet, these initiatives did not try to change the way existing budgets were spent. Rather new, extra, money was parachuted in on top of the old ways of doing things.

First came Urban Aid via the Home Office. Education Priority Areas were designated by the then DfE. Then came Inner City Partnership via the Department of the Environment, City Challenge and, more recently, Single Regeneration and NDC. Each initiative in turn was supposed to change the situation which was generating decay, to change the way local authority specialist departments were organised, to use existing money and effort differently and not simply provide more of the same.

Despite these caring and often imaginative attempts at regeneration, the interests of the institutional silos of central and local government departments and the attitudes of their key players prevailed and the extra cash was used to top up what existed. The result was that the modest funds of £3 or so million a year for each of 3 – 5 years which have been given to troubled areas have provided a few attractive projects, jobs for a few more professionals, the icing on top of a crumbling cake which already cost £100,000,000 each year. It should have been no surprise to discover that, once the funding and the projects ended, the cake continued to crumble and the professionals were deployed elsewhere.

The New Labour Government which was elected in 1997 had the chance to change this situation, provide lasting solutions and bake a new cake. However, the early indications were not good. The Department of Education and Employment introduced the idea of Education Action Zones which include 1 or 2 secondary schools and perhaps a dozen primaries and cover a population of some 15,000 people. The first of these are now underway with more to follow. At the same time, in different neighbourhoods Health, New Deal Community and other Action Zones have also been introduced. No doubt even more zones will follow. Here a zone. There a zone.

All this is all right as far as it goes. But, like their predecessors, the honest intentions of the new government risk being diverted again into icing the crumbling cake instead of helping to bake a new one. None of the education, health and other zones coincide with each other. They are scattered in an ad-hoc way throughout the country. Each one may make a little progress in its specialist area only to be overwhelmed, like previous initiatives, by the other multiple problems which the wider neighbourhood faces. And, remember, while we may end up with, say, 50 EAZs, even 100 Health Zones and 40 NDCs, these will hardly touch the 3,000 troubled neighbourhoods and the 15,000,000 people who live in them.

The joined-up problems which neighbourhoods face can only be tackled by joined-up solutions (see figure 3). It follows that two interlocking changes must be introduced at the same time if government reforms are to work in a lasting and effective way.

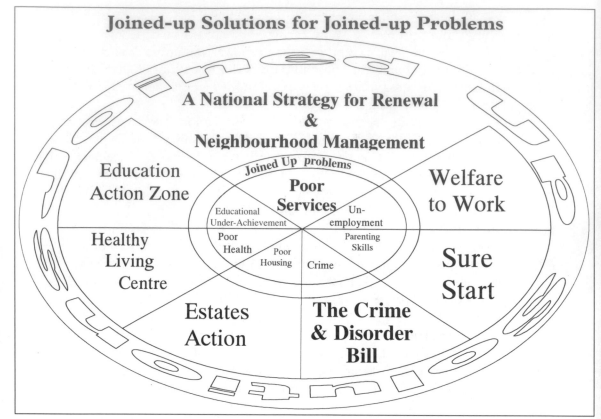

Figure 3

- First, after years of dependency, the response of local people has to be gained, so that they can reach up and grasp the new opportunities presented by devolved budgets and new forms of participation. There is still a long way to go before most people understand the far-reaching implications of fully empowering local residents and the most effective means of doing so.

- Second, Central Government's Departments of State alone can't create and fund enough Zones to produce more than a cosmetic effect on a few neighbourhoods. Government has to devise a way of helping Local Authorities and their existing mainstream budgets to manage and fund all troubled neighbourhoods differently and effectively. The way expensive mainstream services have been provided for such areas must be re-conceived. The reforms already underway in the Welfare State's approach to health, housing, education, benefits, safety etc have to be carried further. They must shift the emphasis from providing things for people to creating the self belief, attitudes and skills needed to enable people to take part in the delivery of the services they need when and how they need them. This does not necessarily require any more money. It does need existing money and budgets to be managed very differently.

To date, we have attempted to kick start sustainable regeneration with only relatively tiny sums on top of unyielding mainstream budgets which have contributed to the problem we are trying to solve. Few experiments yet exist in the serious devolution of taxpayer's funds. But, we must now disassemble that money and reassemble it in fresh ways, which give local people and agencies control and ownership over it.

As with failing schools we now know that inner and outer city areas can't be regenerated by urban aid programs which leave the way they are managed untouched. In future, we must think of regeneration as being inseparable from the reform of the way all welfare services are delivered and urban areas are managed. Regeneration, neighbourhood renewal is not a time-limited programme using external funding. It is good, on going, management. With the help of the Social Exclusion Unit, the government has now accepted this. Its new National Strategy for Neighbourhood Renewal is very promising indeed. It offers the possibility of reaching to the heart of the matter and creating the chance of lasting change during the first decades of the new millennium.

However, many entrenched interests and collective attitudes stand in the way and the government could be deflected by them unless it is very clear about why the reforms are needed and the language through which they are articulated.

The need for a clear rational for reform

The way previous governments have so far spoken about the need for welfare reform has been confusing and unclear. It was first advocated by the Conservative governments of the 80's and attacked by Labour and Liberal Democrat opponents who, as a consequence, have found it difficult to explain why, when in government themselves, they support it.

After releasing the private sector from state control and beginning to ask questions about the value of benefits and pensions, the Conservative governments of the 80's and early 90's began the awesome task of questioning the way major public services were delivered.

Spurred on by the destructive explosions of Handsworth, Brixton and Toxteth in the 1980's, they wondered how schools, houses and other public services such as health could be 'privatised' in order to inject customer demand, choice, self reliance and quality into them in place of supply led mediocrity.

Not only were each of the reforms vigorously opposed by the Labour and the new Liberal Democrat parties, they were also opposed by the many public servants in local authorities, schools, hospitals and elsewhere who were still wedded to the attitude and style of municipal collectivism.

Hence, the only rationale to date for the reform of the Welfare State has been cloaked in the Conservative Government's partial and theoretically derived ideology of 'privatisation.' Many felt it was a euphemism for "individualism, lower taxes and a small or non existent state." The only coherent argument used in opposition to this has been the equally partial ideological and outdated Socialist one which pressed for "higher taxes, more funds and a defence of the Local Authority run school, National Health Service and inner and outer city areas."

This clash of two cultures between Conservative 'Privatisation' and Labour 'Collectivism' has hitherto produced a series of ill considered compromises whose 'raison d'être' owed more to a balance of conflicting powers (a Conservative central government and a Labour local authority) than to a clearly thought out strategy.

This is one reason why the local education authorities resisted the introduction of the local management of schools and why the first EAZs and New Deal Community Pathfinder neighbourhoods were not led by their communities but by the Town Hall. The local politicians and bureaucrats fear and resist change. They can't understand the reasons for it and have no positive and caring picture of where the reforms might be leading.

No practical, ideologically uncontaminated, case for radical social reform has yet been made which could make sense to most people and chart a new, third, path for them to follow. It is essential to do so now if future governments are to succeed in taking these reforms to their logical conclusion, enable whole neighbourhoods to be managed differently and the National Strategy for Renewal to succeed.

Meanwhile, it is vital to note that people in the neighbourhoods we describe have not waited for either government or a new rationale to come to their aid. Without the benefit of this or that ideology or the political correctness of this or that party they have simply started the task of rebuilding their lives. What have they to tell us? Indeed, can they help successive governments to make their case for radical welfare reform compelling, radically distinct from either 'privatisation' and 'nationalisation' and, thus, appealing to most people.

Chapter 5:

Building Communities of Hope

Some people who lived in troubled neighbourhoods could only stand the blight of a post industrial, planning induced, urban decay for a while before shouting. Some shouted very loudly indeed at anyone they could find. But these cries were of frustration and anger. They were negative grumbles. Little happened.

Something more constructive was called for. Some people recognised that "charity begins at home". Unless they did something positive to help themselves nothing would happen.

When this or that person from this or that neighbourhood first decided to call a meeting "to do something about it" (whatever it might be – litter, crime, the need for a youth club) few initially supposed there was any point in braving the apathy of those who had become used to feeling that "nothing can be done." Even to attend took persistence and some courage. Wonderful, noble things have been achieved in situations which appeared to be impossible.

Many of the people who have accomplished the impossible are quite ordinary. They strive to build new associations in an attempt to make life better for their children, relatives and neighbours. Others are professional people whose conventional jobs of priest, head teacher, social worker or housing association director simply could not be done in a conventional way because, respectively, their church was empty, the school was filled with underachievers, their tower block tenants were so numerous that they could not be managed properly in ordinary office hours. Rather than give in, accept second best and opt for a risk free comfortable career some remarkable professionals redefined their job, left their office, found caring, active residents, worked with and empowered them and created new partnerships which made the conventional part of their job more rewarding and productive.

In Balsall Heath such ordinary non party-political residents and professional people were first called Social Entrepreneurs twenty years ago. More recently, in 'Practical People, Noble Causes', Stephen Thake and Charles Leadbeater in 'The Rise of The Social Entrepreneur' have joined with Business in the Community to champion the term and identify a host of people in all four corners of the land who are the pioneers of a silent revolution in which welfare is not delivered only by the State but also by people themselves in close mutual association with each other.

It is common sense, really. The private sector's risk-taking economic entrepreneur earns only if he or she sees a need or a gap in the market and manufactures a product, before marketing and selling it. Some businesses fail because customers won't buy their product. Some succeed wonderfully in building profitable private capital to the benefit of customer, employees and the wider community. The same is true of the social entrepreneur who sees and fills the gap in the social market left by the shrinking family, collapsed local association and long-gone local leaders.

Just as the economic entrepreneur builds financial capital, so the social entrepreneur creates social capital, a home grown alternative to the failing public services of the Welfare State and, thus, is often at first seen as threatening to it. To date, those who have survived and prospered have done so despite rather than because of the 'system'. Because their resident customers have no money and because the defensive state would not devolve its budgets to them, at first the social entrepreneur had to rely on love rather than financial reward or etched out a precarious living from charitable sources.

More recently, however, since the reforms of the 1980's and early 1990's described above, it became possible for social entrepreneurs to find 'real' ways of generating income by trading with the newly devolved budgets of schools, housing associations and the Health Authority.

So, the process of enabling ordinary people to tackle the derelict communities they live in and building caring, sustainable ones in their place has already begun. Social Entrepreneurs have been hard at work helping unconfident residents to manage local community associations for some time.

Indeed, perhaps it is time to move from the term 'Social Entrepreneur' to 'Capacity Builder'. Recent publications have glamorised the Richard Branson-type, charismatic role of the Social Entrepreneur. This image can distract the eye from the fact that rebuilding confidence and associations in areas which have been atrophying for a long time takes time and patience. In particular, it entails passing skills and confidence to unskilled and unconfident people.

This is low-key, almost invisible, work. It is difficult. It takes a very long time and it is most important that the practitioners avoid becoming merely one more indispensable figure who makes local people even more dependant.

The Social Entrepreneur (hereafter, The Capacity Builder) needs a forward and a succession strategy. It is most important that, after any entrepreneurial initiator has long gone, local people say not: "Look what that person did for us," but "Look at what we have done for ourselves."

a) Capacity Building

The need to build the capacity of the community is now appreciated by many people. But few yet know how to achieve it. The interests of the many can be opposed by a few people who resist change. They can be fitted into 4 negative categories:

❏ Criminals.

❏ Local figures who were used to ruling the roost when nobody else was involved, but who can't cope when lots of people are involved.

❏ The professionals, like the teacher who wishes to keep parents out of school because "amateurs have nothing to do with education."

❏ The Councillor who feels threatened if they can't see how bottom-up and top-down can synchronise.

Much time and effort is spent on trying to include everyone by capacity builders. But, despite every patient attempt to involve everyone, one or two people in one or other of these four categories will not want to be included. They will go to considerable lengths to maintain the failing status quo and prevent the inclusion and capacity building of the many.

In order to help the large minority to step to the fore, develop their own voices, build a new array of little associations, it is necessary to hold people in these categories at arms length. That is, one of the most fundamental features of Capacity Building in the creation of **space** for people who are shy, lack skills and the confidence to acquire the ability to shape the quality of their own lives and contribute to the well being of the community.

Another important feature is **time**. The fabric of industrial and post industrial neighbourhoods has been unravelling for 50 years. It will take a generation as well as space to re-knit tattered areas and include excluded people.

To achieve space and time, Capacity Building requires a strong but delicate hand. If the categories described above are to be held at bay while unconfident residents are to find the space and gain the time to build themselves up, then a firm and gentle lead is required. Toughness is needed in keeping the unwanted away, tenderness is required in giving people the long and slow chance to discover their identity and impose it on the public arena.

Even space, time and toughness are not enough. Local people need **resources** if they are to realise their hopes. These include:

❏ **An office** and meeting space. At first an empty shop front, old church hall or flat borrowed from a housing association may suffice. Before long, however, any self-respecting community will need something resembling a village hall in which an array of functions can be held.

❏ **Staff**. Just one Capacity Builder will not satisfy the local appetite for doing things for long. Each neighbourhood will detail its own needs. These might include a number of street caretakers, carers for the elderly, staff for a playgroup, a fund-raiser, negotiator with statutory services, manager of houses leased from the Local Authority – or all of these.

❏ **Assets – property**. A mini-bus and truck might be needed by the caretakers, an old school building by the play-group or carers for the elderly. The users of the park might wish to own it and to reopen a disused church as the focal point of life in the neighbourhood.

❏ And all of these will need the **running costs** which cover heat, light and petrol as well as the salaries of the staff.

With Capacity Building resources such as these, residents who were dependent have come to associate together to form not just 'home-grown' and 'tailor-made' tenants and friendship groups, but nurseries, family centres, job creation schemes and Community Development Trusts which deliver services and welfare on a significant scale. These local, self-help associations which support the unconfident individual and provide them with a springboard to life now exist in every part of the country.

b) Community Sector Trusts and Enterprises

In Liverpool an entire housing estate, the Eldonian Village, complete with a community advice and resource centre, has been built and is run by local people. In Belfast a health centre, shopping complex, housing association, theatre and job creation scheme have been established by the Flax Trust. It has a multi-million pound turnover. In Easterhouse, Glasgow, Bob Holman and colleagues have constructed a wide range of self help associations. The Wise group have generated many dozens of jobs through helping unemployed people to take on services once supplied by statutory service providers. In Bromley by Bow a church now contains a nursery, play group, craft centre and restaurant. By its side is a park, health centre and advice centre. Bromley by Bow has become an urban village. Such villages now exist in most towns and cities in the land.

In Balsall Heath, once Birmingham's red light district, there is:

- An extended-day nursery for children of working parents.

- A secondary school for 70 pupils who have either been excluded from the nearby local authority schools or have excluded themselves.

- A farm and community education resource centre.

- An ecumenical church centre.

- Five mosques and temples which are open 7 days a week.

- A crime reduction scheme which has cut burglaries by 50 per cent and eliminated street corner prostitution.

- A good neighbour scheme which finds, trains and supports 'street stewards' for each street in the area.

- A community newspaper.

- A neighbourhood Forum for the 70 voluntary agencies which have arisen in the last two decades and which liaises with all statutory agencies in what is a prototype of a Composite Action Zone.

- 80 jobs are sustained by these activities and the annual turnover is £2,000,000.

Scattered throughout the country, there are now well over 200 Community Development Trusts or Community Enterprises of the kind outlined above. Some became involved in regeneration principally through education. Others become engaged via job creation, housing or the environment. Most are supported by the national Development Trust Association which has a sister association in Scotland. All end up creating joined-up solutions to a variety of problems regardless of their starting point.

The statistics of the third sector show that it packs a real punch. It accounts for 10% of GDP according to Sir Dennis Landau of the Unity Trust Bank. In Birmingham, Ian Morrison, then Director of its Voluntary Council, showed that 49% of voluntary sector funding is self-generating. The third sector can no longer be depicted as Lady Bountiful confined (by the Welfare State) to the back stage of society. It is now near the centre of the stage and has quietly taken on the provision of excellent welfare services which the state could only struggle to deliver. It is capable of undertaking very much more. It holds the key to the recovery of even the most difficult urban areas. Hitherto, however, the progress and achievements described above have been made against the 'flow' of the Welfare State. It has been made despite, not because of, the way top-down has been organised.

c) Public Sector enterprises

Community enterprises run by Capacity Builders have now been joined by public ones run by Civic Entrepreneurs who enjoy managing the devolved budgets of housing estates, schools and so on. The results they produce can be just as electrifying as those of the Capacity Builder. For example, small groups of schools have begun to cluster together to maximise the use of their new-found budgets, a tendency which is now encouraged by David Blunkett's enthusiasm for Education Action Zones. Some clusters of schools have created a Cluster Facilitator who can help the schools to:

- Save the finance for this key new post within a year by careful planning.
- Undertake joint purchasing from independent suppliers as part of this planning process.
- Gradually increase and manage the range and quality of shared support staff and resources for teachers.
- Gain a greater sense of common purpose, mutual support and high morale.
- Take the strain from head teachers and senior managers.
- Use existing money in innovative ways which enable schools to make the very best of what is available to them.

While different clusters may choose to develop excellence in different curricular areas- arts, technology, science, sports, etc.- they may also choose to achieve a reputation in helping parents to gain the confidence required to give their children the incentive at home to work hard at school.

The pre-school teacher can be a vital link between the floundering mother and father and others in the community who can help. The school and its neighbours could build nurseries. Toy, book and resource libraries could help show parents how to talk to and care for their children. Other parents can offer support as well as ideas and suggestions for everything from healthy diet to the best means of controlling difficult behaviour.

The primary school, like the doctor's surgery or health centre, is a natural meeting place for parents of young children – they go there frequently. Indeed, in some places, the surgery and health centre could also be integrated within the school to form a 'Family Centre'. The more prepared the young child becomes in its preschool years, the more the school can make rapid progress when the child starts its formal school life. In return the more the child is able to progress at school, the more the parent is able to cope and help the child to make progress at home.

Thus, it is possible to envisage the nursery and primary school as being not just the 'provider' of education to young children but also a centre for the whole family. Indeed, the nursery and primary school could combine the functions of education with those of social and health care, advice and training in parenting and employment skills.

To facilitate and accommodate the Family Centre, each nursery and primary school only needs a modest suite of rooms in which the roles of the priest, teacher, social worker, doctor and policeman can intertwine. Indeed, the Family Centre could become the focal point for a kind of informal college of life-long learning and mutual support for the entire neighbourhood.

Some schools, especially secondary schools, have become very enterprising. The Garibaldi school near Nottingham under the leadership of Sir Bob Salisbury raises funds by letting its premises as a conference centre. Others now do outside catering as an extension of food technology and help to train trainee teachers. This is only the start of what is possible.

There is an interesting alternative to schools using a small but significant part of each school's budget to buy in independent suppliers in order to provide themselves with such services as grounds maintenance, buildings maintenance, painting and decorating, printing, catering and so on. They could start their own Local Education Enterprises Company (LEEC) and use it to supply these services themselves. Housed in local premises, like the old nursery school which one of Birmingham's clusters uses, a cluster's LEEC could fulfil several purposes. It might for example:

- Provide good, homegrown, services.

- Keep the costs of those services within the cluster by funding the LEEC.

- Create local jobs.

- Use those jobs as 'education-by-doing' devices to guide work experience placements from years 10 and 11 and to help school leavers to transition from welfare to work projects into real jobs.

● The local college is likely, for instance, to run courses in bricklaying, painting and decorating and so on, but to have few real outlets for their trainees to practice on with lasting effect. The cluster of local schools and other voluntary associations are obvious locations on which trainees and apprentices can work, so building the pride which comes from gainful employment.

A cluster of schools which runs a successful 'LEEC Plc' need not stop at sharing services which its members need. It could supply services to other players in its catchment area, such as housing associations and businesses. A state school or cluster of schools which operates in this enterprising way could soon match the investment and endowment funds which private schools use to give bursaries or build a new science block or swimming pool. Once released from the dependent, one-dimensional mode of thought of the top-down pyramid, in which schools receive orders and do not set fresh visions for what is possible, the sky becomes the limit.

Just as Capacity Builders and Community Development Trusts can attack bottom-up regeneration from any one of a number of starting points, so also self-governing schools, housing associations and compacts between any one of them and the police or health authority can have a similar top-down outcome.

The really exciting prospect, however, is to link together the distinct bottom-up and top-down input of the Capacity Builder and Civic Entrepreneur, their Community Development Trust and self-governing public agency. Hitherto, this has happened only rarely and as a result of accident rather than design. It is time to remedy this defect in order to provide once troubled neighbourhoods with the social capital and vibrant hinterland of close at home mutual associations and the assets of professional people, buildings and land which are vital if they are to become viable. This is the far reaching direction in which the hesitant welfare reforms of the last two decades could now be taken. How do we build on what has already been achieved, multiply the good news story and make progress in the future both more straightforward and easier?

Chapter 6:

Neighbourhood Management

If we rely on a few visionary Capacity Builders and Civic Entrepreneurs to rebuild our 3,000 troubled neighbourhoods we will have to wait a long time and progress will be sporadic. The time-scale will be considerably shortened and results will be more universal if we rearrange and improve the way statutory services are delivered to neighbourhoods so that the expensive welfare system pulls with and enables the entrepreneur and neighbourhood.

The changes required are substantial and varied. But a significant set of foundation stones can be best subsumed under the title Neighbourhood Management. The main components of Neighbourhood Management are:

- The geographically defined neighbourhood itself.
- Community ownership and the Capacity Builder.
- The Neighbourhood Development Plan.
- Reopening failed services under the new management of a senior neighbourhood officer or civic entrepreneur and their inter departmental neighbourhood team.
- Finance.
- Top-down and bottom-up partnerships.

a. Neighbourhoods.

- Each local authority contains many neighbourhoods or urban villages. Yet, most of these have 'sunk' beneath the urban sprawl and are criss-crossed by planning and service delivery lines. These neighbourhoods, none-the-less usually have names – Headingly, Handsworth, Toxteth. The people who live in them identify with them. For them, they are home.

- Neighbourhoods can be of mixed or local authority housing, as small as 2,000 people or as large as 20,000 and there are thousands of them in the country. Birmingham has 85, Walsall 55, Liverpool 70.

- The first remedial task to undertake is to enable local people to gather together, and define the area in which they live, much like villages of old 'beat their bounds.' How can revitalised communities be given an outward expression? How can the many urban villages from which each town is built, be excavated from beneath the accumulated concrete jungle and exert their identity upon the physical, social and economic geography of tomorrow? The following suggestions form only a brief introductory answer which might begin to name and assert the sense of place and identity of each neighbourhood or urban village.

- As the charity Common Ground has shown, urban villages need to mark their boundaries, with clear entry and exit points. There is sense in making these obvious and distinctive, like postal district signs so that residents and visitors can know when they are being 'welcomed' within these boundaries or invited to return upon leaving. They also need a central focal point. It does not matter whether the centre is identified by shops, a library, a school or community centre as long as it is clear to residents where this centre is, and as long as it has the right atmosphere, either because of its architecture or the quality of the services which it offers or both. Perhaps a distinctive flag, crest or shield might help to give identity to both the entry gateways and the central features of the village.

- At Christmas, Diwali, Eid, carnival time or during some other local celebration, both gateways and central features might be enhanced by festive decorations, perhaps prepared by schools, or religious organisations, residents' groups or other voluntary organisations. The content and style of the celebrations will, of course, differ according to the particular community. But, whatever their content, they are important occasions and the more people that take part in the planning and execution the better. Such occasions can represent the strength of the community in a variety of forms including sport, art and business as well as being purely social or religious events. They can serve to highlight calendar festivals and mark the natural passing of the seasons which urban life otherwise obscures.

- A building which functions as a village hall and meeting place and the open space which represents the village green or some kind of arena are important, not only to host celebrations but to serve the needs of different interest groups. Community notice boards and community newspapers can advertise events and spread local news and information, providing the village with its own voice while also helping to promote local businesses and schools. A supplement to the newspaper might form a 'welcome package' for those moving into the area and introduce them to the local amenities and their neighbours.

- As Lord Rodger's report, "Towards Urban Renaissance", indicates, buildings and developments which affect the life of the village often do not take enough account of its particular identity or of the wishes of residents. It would be profitable to build and develop in ways which highlight that identity rather than inhibit, depress or destroy it. The style and proportions of buildings, the materials used and the locations of facilities are all crucial to the creation of harmony in a neighbourhood as well as a sense of history, continuity and belonging.

b. Community Ownership and the Capacity Builder.

Bounds can't be beaten unless the people who live within them do so. If the land, buildings and people within these bounds are to be cared for, maintained and sustained then it is the people who live there who will do it. And, if they are to achieve this, then they will need all the Capacity Building, offices, staff and resources described in the previous chapter. In addition, they will need a 'voice'. The capacity builder, their staff and resources will need to be accountable to a Forum of residents who are in some way representative of their neighbourhood. This Neighbourhood Forum will not only manage the staff but prepare an agenda for local action and advocate it both locally and to statutory agencies.

c. The Neighbourhood Development Plan.

No self respecting business in the private sector would dream of trading without the guidance of a Business Development Plan. (And no self respecting banker would lend a business money unless they had studied the plan and seen that it was realistic). Recently school managers have discovered the need for each school to have a School Development Plan which reviews progress and targets on a year on year basis.

It is common sense really, as well as good business practice, for each neighbourhood to work out a Neighbourhood Development Plan or its residents and the agencies which service them will not know what targets they are aiming to achieve, whether they are falling short or improving, what they are costing or if they are worth it.

Each Neighbourhood Development Plan will need to be ambitious if it aims to turn the whole area round within, say, five years and then sustain progress. It will need to address all of the following subjects and set ambitious targets:

- *Defining the neighbourhood.* Drawing the boundary of the neighbourhood in social and communal and not planning terms suggests the need to reorder political, city department, police and other lines to conform with that boundary – no easy task. Even with the help of a Capacity Builder the process may take 2 or 3 years before it is complete. But, it is an essential first step before a failing neighbourhood can be fully recovered. The nationally based Boundary Commissioners will help, for it is their task to agree local ward and parliamentary boundaries.

- *The family* is the basis of the community and the living springboard from which the child leaps into adult maturity and independence. Families which are not fortunate enough to have more than one voice and one pair of hands, who cannot benefit from the wisdom of uncles, aunts and grandparents can be substantially helped by neighbours and more experienced parents. Schemes like Home-Start and Sure Start help to organise mature parents to assist those who are as yet disorganised and risk giving inconsistent, contradictory messages to their impressionable child.

- *Good physical and mental health* is essential if the family is to be cared for and the individual to be economically and socially self-reliant and benefit from, as well as contribute to, a spirited communal life. Prevention is better than cure. Yet, the disproportionately high child death rate, the death of adults from heart disease, etc., causes both an economic and emotional drain on the typical neighbourhood of despair. Alongside the medical practice and hospital bed, adequate care in the community measures and healthy living centres are needed, which encourage people to lead a healthier, more robust, life-style.

- *The house or flat* needs to be bright, secure, have a front door which is personal and private, be well-maintained and have an entry way and private or shared garden which is attractive and generates pride. Private ownership encourages the sense of responsibility to care for the premises and make it suitable for a thriving family life. When ownership is public and, therefore, shared, each individual should be able to become personally involved and influence the way their property is managed. Priority Estates Planning and others have pioneered tenant management of tower and low-rise blocks. They illustrate the many benefits which can accrue from tenants managing their own housing stock.

- *The School* boosts or blights the child's life chances as much as does the family. The previous chapter illustrated the way the good school or cluster of schools can support both child, parent and community.

- *Employment* both engenders dignity and provides the individual with the ability to support themselves and their dependents. It enables the individual not to be a drain on finances, but to pay taxes which help both the Exchequer and those who have fallen on hard times. Good schooling and training is one answer. So is New Deal, work experience and the creation of Community Enterprises. Manufacturing industries will continue to shrink and technology alone cannot sustain high/full employment. In future, the service industries will continue to grow as will the need to care for an ever-increasing elderly population. The third sector is a growth industry whose job creation potential is yet to be fully explored.

- *Community safety* is the key to an improving quality of life. The police spend 98% of their budget and manpower on detecting crime. But, they achieve the prosecution of only 3% of offenders. Yet, they only spend 2% of their budget on preventing the 97% of offenders who are not prosecuted from committing an offence. Of course, conventional arrests must be encouraged. But, as innovative schemes like <u>restorative justice</u> and <u>neighbourhood</u> wardening illustrate, community involvement and preventative policing can reduce crime dramatically.

- *The built and green environment* gives an enduring impression to the growing child and can, when properly stewarded, lift the spirit of the adult. Does it go without saying that the building, park or gutter which is owned by and the clear responsibility of a local individual or agency will be maintained, while the one which is not will not be tended?

- *Diverse Mutual Community Associations and Enterprises* will be created in all the arenas of neighbourhood life described above. Some of these will be purely voluntary; some will employ staff and, thus, create jobs; others, perhaps one or two per neighbourhood, will be sophisticated Community Trusts with a significant financial turnover. These will trade with and relate to self-governing statutory agencies – schools, housing associations, etc.

- *These bottom-up solutions are joined-up* and they all correspond to one or other top-down government Initiative. Alone, each of these distinct features of the plan is not sufficient to achieve sustainable change. It is crucial that they are all tackled and managed together as vital parts of an integrated whole.

- *Quality Review and Inspection.* All the above activities and targets should, as with any Development Plan, be reviewed on a year on year basis and updated accordingly. The Local Police and other agencies will wish to ensure that standards are set and achieved, to intervene where they are not and to reward where they are exceeded. Good practice should be disseminated from neighbourhood to neighbourhood and from Authority to Authority.

If, as figure 4 depicts, the ambitious targets in each neighbourhood's plan outlines are achieved then, in a few short years, it should be possible to turn a failing area round in just the same way we now know a failing school can be saved. All that is required is:

- A budget

- Good management by one Capacity Builder and one Civic Entrepreneur- and support staff.

- Clear sighted aims and targets

- Enthusiasm and will

- Inspection, sanction and praise by the local authority and resident's forum.

Chart of Neighbourhood Development Plan.

Area	Key Players	Target	Review date
The family	All relevant agencies and key resident representatives	Help, say, 100 families. Create parent centres in every primary school	In 12 months time
Health	All relevant agencies and key resident representatives	Reduce infant mortality by 20%. Set up, healthy living centres	In 12 months time
The House	All relevant agencies and key resident representatives	Involve all tenants in management of the house	In 12 months time
The school	All relevant agencies and key resident representatives	Improve standard by 30%. Cluster and pool resources	In 12 months time
Employment	All relevant agencies and key resident representatives	Reduce unemployment by 50%	In 12 months time
Crime	All relevant agencies and key resident representatives	Reduce crime by 50%	In 12 months time
The environment	All relevant agencies and key resident representatives	Clear the litter remove the graffiti	In 12 months time
Mutual associations	All relevant agencies and key resident representatives	Enable all the residents to help each other at a very local level	In 12 months time
Assets	All relevant agencies and key resident representatives	Take ownership of key parks, lands and buildings	In 12 months time
Neighbourhoods management	All relevant agencies and key resident representatives	All key agencies to be actively involved	In 12 months time
Partnership between residents and statutory agencies	All relevant agencies and key resident representatives	The bottom-up and top-down to be playing fully to each others strengths	In 12 months time
Quality review and inspection	All relevant agencies and key resident representatives	Set new plan and new targets in 1 years time. Identify strengths and weaknesses	In 12 months time

Figure 4

- Perhaps later years and stages (2, 3 or 4) of the Neighbourhood Development Plan will take in the ownership and management of real assets by local people. This will include land, buildings and, above all, the employment of local people.

- *When, and if,* this advanced stage is reached, some Neighbourhood Forums, associations, enterprises and trusts may well themselves take on the delivery of such key services as:

  - Care in the community
  - Some other Social Services such as elderly day care
  - Some Leisure Services
  - Schools
  - Houses
  - Environmental works
  - Community enterprises and job creation.

d. The Senior Neighbourhood Manager and the Neighbourhood Team.

- Some 15 years ago the educational establishment was horrified to discover that HMG had approved the Local Management (LM) of all state schools.

- As discussed, before then, nobody knew what an individual school budget was. Even a broken door knob or window had to be requisitioned from the LEA. A central committee of 15 councillors 'managed' all the schools in their area. LEA's did not savour the loss of control. Heads had never handled more than dinner money. There was much anxiety and confusion.

- Today, more than 90% of heads value LM and self-government. They can target their budgets to the exact point of the chalk face that needs it. Windows are now mended quickly. Each school's governing body of 15 plus does just that, it governs.

- Yet, it is astonishing to recall that the failing neighbourhoods we wish to regenerate do not have defined boundaries. No one knows what sums are poured into them by the statutory agencies. There is nobody who is collectively responsible for them. That is, the £100,000,000 which is spent on the typical neighbourhood of 15,000 people is not managed at all. Quite literally it is spent without account.

- It follows that in addition to a Capacity Builder, Neighbourhood Forum and Development Plan each troubled neighbourhood also needs a senior Neighbourhood Manager who will be responsible for discussing what these sums are, the quality of the services delivered by them and the new targets needed to improve them year on year.

- A Neighbourhood Manager might be appointed or seconded from the ranks of local authority officers or, as with some managers of EAZ's, they might come from outside the local authority.

- Indeed, it is important that many come from industry, the police or health professionals to whom they will have to relate just as directly as any local authority department.

- It is important to remember that 3,000 plus of these senior managers will eventually be needed, one for each neighbourhood. It will not be easy to identify, recruit, train and support so many, especially as they will have to be independent spirits able to rise to daunting challenges and to manage themselves as well as their inner-agency neighbourhood team. Someone previously trapped and frustrated within the Local Authority may surprise us all. Equally, someone experienced in setting-up and running the new branch of an expanding business may have a head start.

- Crucially, from the word 'go', the Senior Manager will need to think in new ways, bang established heads together, assemble an inter-agency team of players able to help the Capacity Builder and Forum to deliver the Neighbourhood Development Plan, meet and improve upon ambitious targets.

- Education Action Zones have an educational supremo who is valued at £60/70k. The head of a secondary school with a budget of £2.5m can earn £60k. The Manager of a neighbourhood on which £100m is spent should be paid £80k or more. The right calibre of person must be attracted and all concerned must know that they have the stature, status and determination to succeed where all others have not even tried.

- The senior neighbourhood manager of statutory services will wish to:

  - Work closely with his/her Capacity Builder counterpart. Together, they are the flip sides of the coin of neighbourhood management.
  - Assist The Forum with the annual preparation and review of the neigh-bourhood development plan.
  - Ensure that the statutory components and targets of that plan are hit and improved upon.
  - Enable the Community's Capacity Builder and local associations to trade with devolved statutory services and, where appropriate, undertake some of these services.
  - Help the Local Authority to move from a situation where the community sector is dependent on time-limited grants and regeneration initiatives to one where they can trade with the public and private sectors, build sustainable community enterprises, jobs and a vibrant hinterland.

- Report to a delivery board which is community led by the Neighbourhood Forum.

- The Senior Manager will need to choose an inter-agency Neighbourhood Team of officers from amongst the existing staff of different departments and ensure that they both play to each other's strengths and those of the community.

- At first, this team may well help existing specialist service providers to improve the quality of that provision. By degrees, however, a number of these services may be sensibly passed to the community to deliver. Schools are now controlled by Governors drawn from the local area and many housing estates are managed by tenants. The question to ask, therefore, is not which services might be passed to local people to manage, but which should not be delivered in this way.

e. The 'top down' and the 'bottom up' are interdependent

- Some professionals and policy makers have suggested that it is sufficient to reorganise the top-down into the neighbourhood management teams described. These, it is said, will deliver the goods and that a new form of bottom-up response from the community is unnecessary and too prescriptive. Why should communities be expected and encouraged to behave with such a degree of responsibility?

- This question is ill-considered. It does not make practical sense. Even the most sensitive and caring service which is delivered 'for' people still makes them dependent and unable to help themselves. It de-skills and de-motives them. It conveys the message: 'You have rights, but no responsibilities.'

- Thus, it makes the task of even the well motivated professional difficult if not impossible and further atrophies the spirit and quality of life in neighbourhoods.

- If inner and outer city areas are to recover and if people are to be empowered to take control of and shape their lives, then sophisticated new forms of local mutual associations and participatory representation are quite essential ingredients of a new top-down, bottom-up partnership. That is, **the flip side of the coin of the civic entrepreneur and neighbourhood management is the Capacity Builder who** forges and fastens the communal bonds within the neighbourhood and makes it responsive to well delivered neighbourhood services to the point where some of these are delivered by local people. (see figure 5)

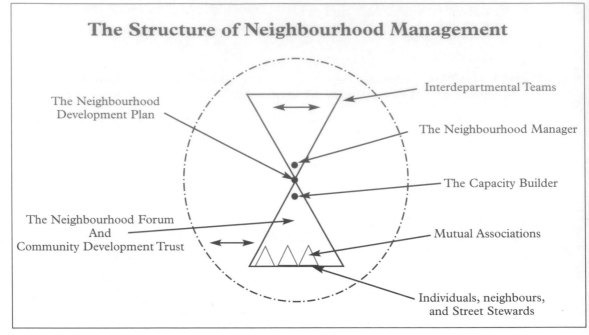

The Structure of Neighbourhood Management

Interdepartmental Teams

The Neighbourhood
Development Plan

The Neighbourhood Manager

The Capacity Builder

The Neighbourhood Forum
And
Community Development Trust

Mutual Associations

Individuals, neighbours,
and Street Stewards

Figure 5

f. The perils of the Neighbourhood Board

In the wake of the nationally unfurling National Strategy for Neighbourhood Renewal it will be all too easy for the local authority and other professionals to forget the need for this partnership and, in haste, proceed with Neighbourhood Teams and senior Neighbourhood Officers before the community within the neighbourhood is prepared.

If past experience is anything to go by, the professional will set up a Neighbourhood Board to manage the Senior Officer and team and will, no doubt, feel it is sufficient to involve 'the community' by inviting a few residents to sit on it. However:

- Even when significant numbers of residents/local businesses are on such a Local Authority devised Neighbourhood Board, the minutes, papers, agendas and committee procedures puzzle them and make them feel that they are unequal partners.

- The professional's language and familiarity with procedures and bids can overcome the local voice.

- Big players have big agendas and are well practised at securing their objectives although these have, in the past, often been part of the problem which residents face.

- Community representatives are very slow off the mark because they lack both experience and confidence. In the past, by the time residents have got their act together, professionals have snapped up all the opportunities.

- Thus, even with Neighbourhood Boards which give the impression of local involvement, there is a real danger that the services will still fail to produce the best results because they do not allow for the kind of local ownership and pride which are essential for sustainability. Residents will not respond to them as if they were theirs.

g. A Neighbourhood Trust

In place of an officer dominated Neighbourhood Board which is set up too quickly for residents to control, an independent community led Neighbourhood Trust is needed.

Many of the larger voluntary organisations which were described earlier are set up as Development Trusts and are either or both charities and Limited Companies. The residents who Chair and manage these trusts find the task no more or less arduous than chairing or sitting on a School's Board of Governors.

So, it makes sense to suggest that when their confidence has been built, the residents of each neighbourhood might form a Neighbourhood Trust, register it as a charity, Limited Company or both and invite the Neighbourhood Manager, a local Councillor and one or two other key players to join it on their terms. Not 'crumbs from the table' or 'sitting at the table' but 'owning the table and setting the agenda.'

Despite previous suggestions by government that the community might lead on SRB bids, out of 373 initiatives only 8 had residents to the fore. If this statistic is to be reversed, then government will have to be even more directive than has previously been the case.

It may be, of course, that residents do not wish to proceed entirely on their own but in partnership with others who may include any one or more of the private sector, BitC, the Police, PCG or Local Authority.

Either way, it is the Trust and not the Local Authority which should employ the Senior Neighbourhood Manager, be responsible for holding the various statutory agencies to account for delivering their part of the Neighbourhood Development Plan and allocating the resources needed to maintain the work of the Capacity Builder and Neighbourhood Forum.

h. The costs of Capacity Building and Neighbourhood Management.

The minimal initial additional Cost of the Community's capacity Builder and the Senior Neighbourhood Manager can be summarised as follows:

1. The initial needs of the Community Forum

Bottom-up

• Forum	The Capacity Builder (Social Entrepreneur)	50
	Sec/Admin	25
	Safety	19
	Environment	19
	Special projects	70
	Running Costs	20
	Total	£203k

2. The needs of the Neighbourhood's Management Team

Top-Down

• Neighbourhood Management	Senior Manager (civic entrepreneur)	80
	Secretary	15
	Team identified from within all relevant departments	–
	Running Costs	35
	Total	£130k
	Total	**£333k**

In addition to these initial costs those of essential developments should be considered. These will include a Community Enterprise, Street Stewards and Staffing Structures.

Every row of houses contains at least one Good Neighbour or Street Warden who can provide for a range of activities - advice, parenting skills, first aid, safety, care for the elderly etc. In an area of, say, 5,000 dwellings and 15,000 residents there might be 60 streets.

If the Street Stewards of each set of 20 streets associate together to manage their own little task force of Caretaker and health workers, a base and material resources, then wonders could be achieved. Thus, the area might have 3 sets of staff each covering 20 streets and a co-ordinator, secretary and assistant to help the residents and their Capacity Builder to ensure effective delivery. The structure can be depicted and costed as follows:

3. The needs of a community enterprise

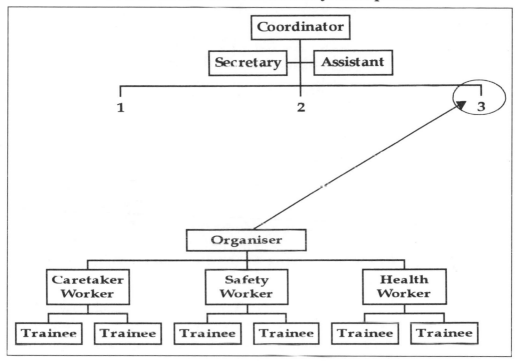

The Cost of these 3 coordinated teams might equal:

Revenue

Co-ordinator and Assistant	At 25 + 20	£45k
Secretary	15	£15k
Organiser x 3	12	£36k
Caretaker Warden x 3	10	£30k
Safety x 3	10	£30k
Health x 3	10	£30k
Trainees x 60 running costs	15	£15k
		£201k

Capital

X3 Trucks	At 10	£30k

Summary of costs:

Capacity builder	203
Neighbourhood Management	130
Community enterprise	201
Capital	30

Revenue total = £534k. Capital total £30k

In their powerfully argued book titled Neighbourhood Management, Anne Power and Emmet Bergin suggest that the cost of staff needed to service each neighbourhood might be of the following order:

Budget for Neighbourhood Management

1. *for an area of 1000 units, excluding housing or other services costs, but including super-caretaking/warden services to provide a custodial/maintenance/liaison/ support/service*

Neighbourhood Management	£35,000
Administrative/community support	£16,000
Office costs	£5,000
Employer costs (at 20%)	£10,200
Super-caretaker/wardens (1 per 200 properties including on-costs)	£100,000
Equipment and materials	£10,000
Community fund (for small local initiatives and pump-priming)	£20,000
TOTAL	**£196,200**

Cost per unit = £196 per household; £78 per person

2. *for an area of 4500 units as above*

Function	Cost
Neighbourhood Manager	£60,000
Admin./PA	£18,000
Community support manager	£30,000
Admin./Organiser	£16,000
Supervision of environmental service delivery (2 posts)	£50,000
On-costs at 20%	£34,800
Super-caretaker/wardens (1 per 200 + supervisors – 24 posts)	£480,000
Materials and equipment	£25,000
Office costs	£90,000
Community fund (£20 per household p.a.)	£90,000
TOTAL	£848,800

Cost per unit = £189 per annum; £76 per person

The authors total of £434,000 represents less than 0.5% of the existing welfare spending in a neighbourhood of 15,000 people. Anne Power and Emmet Bergin's costs for neighbourhoods of 1000 units (3,000 people) and 4,500 units (13,500 people) are a little more, nearly 1%. In particular, they show how their costs can be funded from the revenue made from houses in a municipal estate. In areas of mixed housing the funds would have to come not just from Housing Associations but also from other authority departments, health and police funds. The advantages to these agencies are clear. That is, once Capacity Building and Neighbourhood Management are underway these costs can and should be found by rearranging the way existing welfare funds are spent. They should not come from external, time limited, grants.

i. Meeting the costs of Neighbourhood Management

- The Treasury is now examining just how much money goes into each urban neighbourhood every year. Its conclusions are still unclear. Supposing at the end of the day it is the £100 million which this author has suggested, then it bears repetition that between just 0.5% and 1% would be sufficient to fund the bottom up initiative of the Capacity Builder, the Neighbourhood Manager and neighbourhood team and give them teeth.

- It will be necessary to look more carefully at these percentages. Whatever figures are settled on, as with schools, a national funding formula arrangement will have to be agreed which enables the Neighbourhood Management costs of different neighbourhoods to be dealt with in the same clear way.

- However, it would be unwise to tackle all 3,000 neighbourhoods at once. To date, we have too few, if any, models of good practice in which both skilled Capacity Building and Neighbourhood Management are working in tandem. We need, say, 50/100 good working models within a year or two.

- Then, as each year goes by, we need to take in another set. If, say, we tackle 200 a year, we will begin work in all 3000 in 15 years.

- Each neighbourhood will need the start-up funds outlined for Capacity Building and Management funds from Central Government for a couple of years. But these sums should be made conditional upon all local statutory partners agreeing to begin to disassemble their own funds and take on the necessary payments thereafter.

- With this in mind it is possible to calculate from the costs of starting Capacity Building and Neighbourhood Management in each area the overall costs for the Treasury.

- Noting that each neighbourhood will initially cost around £500,000 for each of 2 years making a total of £1m, then all 3,000 areas will cost £3,000 million over 15 years. The costs per year equal £150m. Given that just 40 NDC areas are costing £800m to fund just 40 neighbourhoods, this is very cheap at the price. Indeed, the sum needed by the whole nation each year is only equal to the total costs going into just one and a half neighbourhoods each and every year.

j. A library of experience and ideas

Not long ago, only residents in neighbourhoods where capacity building was well advanced sung the praises of Neighbourhood Management arguing that without it large sums of taxpayers money were being inadequately squandered. More recently, a number of well considered studies have confirmed the practical experience of residents and practitioners and put their distinct features together into a composite whole.

David Wilkinson and his colleague the Rev Applebae wrote **Implementing Holistic Government.** Perri 6 wrote **Holistic Government** and, with colleagues, **Governing in the round**. Marilyn Taylor's **Top-Down meets Bottom-Up** was published by The Rowntree Foundation. Anne Power and Emmet Bergin published **Neighbourhood Management**. The Social Exclusion Unit's Policy Action team 4 produced a government-approved portrait of **Neighbourhood Management** which is the hub around which the **National Strategy for Neighbourhood Renewal** turns. These documents and others lend authority to the view which practitioners had worked out in the light of experience.

In her important book Top Down meets Bottom Up, Marilyn Taylor points out that while there are almost no polished, long standing, instances of Neighbourhood Management as outlined in these pages, many different pieces of the jig-saw can be found in different parts of the country. Indeed, she provides many convincing and successful illustrations which include a local housing company in Poples which was created by the voluntary transfer of stock from Tower Hamlets Borough Council. This company has created an income stream for community regeneration of £100 per tenant which adds up to £800,000 per year which would easily pay for the costs outlined above.

Other examples which arise from non-housing initiatives in mixed tenure areas can be found in Coventry, Walsall, the North East, Sandwell and Kirklees. All boast that key components of Neighbourhood Management are already in place and working well.

Building the Capacity of the community, the Neighbourhood Forum, the introduction of Neighbourhood Management, the role of the Senior Neighbourhood Manager and the Neighbourhood Development Trust and the adequate financing of these are essential features of renewal. But, alone, they are not the whole of it. The next essential ingredient which we must consider is the issue of accountability.

Some are anxious that devolving budgets and services to a 'lower' level attacks the democratic principle and creates a deficit at the heart of democracy. The very opposite is true. But, to demonstrate this we must examine the relationship between participatory democracy and the representative kind. For, both form the context within which Neighbourhood Management must work if it is to succeed.

Renewal: The Passage of Time

The way we were in 1970

Kite flying diverts the eye from the reality on the ground and in the home.

YOU ARE NOW ENTERING A JOB FREE ZONE!

But, without a job to look forward to, it is difficult to find much motivation at school....... or anywhere else!

Bleak horizons just half a mile from the town centre depress the soul and the economy. A criminal culture can seem appealing.

Vulnerable girls can be pulled into prostitution and boys into becoming 'apprentice' pimps and drug pushers. Thus, criminals take over the streets and residents are faced with these options: Move. Stay and accept. Or, stay and change things – if you can.

The fight can begin anywhere.

In this particular case, it was the sight of this stairway – the back entrance to the local college.

Youngsters who went there felt ashamed. The stairway could be seen from the main road.

They painted out the shame and felt better, proud even.

The idea can
be catching.

People ask:

"Why . . .

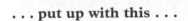

. . . put up with this . . .

. . . when it can look like this?"

The answer is obvious.
It's common sense really.

The 'Urban jungle' has more than one meaning. Once the graffiti and rubbish collect outside the front door, it is easy to let the back door slip.

With the right attitude, its just as easy to recover the lost ground – and create jobs. Agencies will pay to have graffiti and rubbish removed. Housing Associations and others will pay for gardens to be maintained. As they say: 'Where there's muck there's brass' – and jobs.

Going, Going. . .

Gone!

Even the largest challenges can be met. This block was opened by Harold
Wilson in 1963. He declared it to be: "The New Jerusalem". By 1993 it had
become a municipally designed disaster area which the residents insisted
was knocked down. When it was, they raised the flag, then invited a
Housing Association to build family style houses.

Even street corner prostitution, kerb-crawling and drugs can be ended.

When residents shamed the 'demand' away the 'supply' dwindled to nothing.

Residents explain their tactics to their Chief Constable with the help of their Councillors. Their partnership with the private sector is strengthened by one with the police.

Again, jobs can be created – in sign making, and making the streets safer. Insurance companies will reduce premiums if there are fewer break-ins to houses and businesses.

For actions to succeed, discussion is required. The partners – residents, voluntary organisations, businesses, the police, health and local authority – need to compare notes. It is best done with colour, entertainment and an agenda prepared by residents.

The best ideas – and real understanding and friendship – can arise over a meal. At this meeting one resident said: "We've stopped the graffiti and rubbish, built houses and ended prostitution. We now know we can do anything we want."

Mothers can plan a surer start in school life for their children.

The new generation can landscape the once rubble strewn park, then entertain their friends.

O.K. so, we have done that. What's next?

How about:
Our own playcentre and swings, built by our dads!

Faith (and flags) can move mountains.

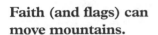

The vision of a better quality of life is limited not by material conditions but by the imagination.

Rome was not built in a day . . . it took time.

But it's such fun getting there.

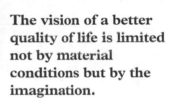

Just reach for the sky.

The smiles tell the story of success.

Let a thousand flowers bloom.

The way we are heading in 2000.

BALSALL HEATH FORUM

Chapter 7:

Adding Participatory Democracy to the Representative kind

The credibility gap between the people and the politicians who have provided the one-size-fits-all services of the Welfare State has become worryingly large, especially at the level of local government. So, the implications of new, resilient, neighbourhoods for the strengthening of the democratic process are encouraging. The gap could be bridged.

However, progress can only be made if we accept that the representative way by which the existing system of welfare is held to account has become as inadequate to today's world as the mine and cotton mill of yesteryear. It is now out of synchronisation with where people are and what urban regeneration requires. It can't deliver what people yearn for – a better, inclusive, life for their children.

Representative Democracy

Today, representative democracy gives all people over 18 the vote. The vote is exercised once a year in local Council elections when the voter elects one of three Councillors for a three year period and once every five years in General Elections when an MP is elected.

This right to vote for a person from a political party who will represent the voter for 3-5 years, was hard won. Women had to chain themselves to railings and go to prison to achieve it. People who did not own property had to campaign for it. More recently, the vote was given to all 18 year olds. So, representative democracy has evolved and changed. It is still changing. Soon, the first past the post system may be reformed to make way for proportional representation.

Representative democracy is good. It was a very great advance on what went before when only one powerful land owning aristocratic class had access to power and the levers of government.

But, it also has its draw-backs, especially in today's age of instant communication where the voter knows as much, if not more, than the politician, where so many events are beyond the ability of the politician to influence, where ordinary people are no longer happy to accept state provided one-size-fits-all services because they have learned from the manufacturing world the virtues of choice and diversity and the power they can command over the quality of what is on offer.

The Draw Backs

Each Local Council ward has a voting population of about 25,000 people. A Parliamentary Constituency can contain 65,000 people. Respectively, what do the voters do for the next three and five years after they have elected their representative? Politically and practically speaking, they do nothing.

Further, voters do not select the politicians who they can vote for. They are chosen by party activists of whom there are very few. So, voters can't vote for whom they choose. Their choice is limited to one of three people from three political parties selected by the activists.

Worse still, in some areas, less than 20% of the voters vote in local elections (72% in general ones). Of these, up to 49% vote for the candidate who is not selected. So, less than 10% vote for the selected person. That is, 90% plus do not get the person they want! This country, in particular it's inner and outer city areas, compares very unfavourably with others. See figure 6.

TURNOUT IN RECENT LOCAL ELECTIONS ACROSS EUROPE

LUXEMBOURG	93%
SWEDEN	90%
ITALY	85%
BELGIUM	80%
DENMARK	80%
GERMANY	72%
FRANCE	70%
SPAIN	64%
IRELAND	62%
PORTUGAL	60%
NETHERLANDS	54%
POLAND	43%
U.K.	40%
WALSALL M. B. C.	25%
MANY INNER AND OUTER CITY NEIGHBOURHOODS	18%

Figure 6

Once elected, Councillors then go to the Town Hall to manage the large bureaucracies of City Departments and follow their party line. MPs do likewise in Whitehall. The effect that either has over the voter's home, family, street, park, school, job is minimal. Their contact with the voter or neighbourhood between elections is non-existent.

Yet, we now have more Councillors and MPs and the Town Hall and Whitehall are bigger now than when the country governed 50% of the whole world 100 years ago.

"In political terms, the creation of the Welfare State saw the triumph of representative democracy over civic democracy in personal welfare, housing, education, health and the general environment." In other words, Frank Prochaska argues in the IEA's publication, Involuntary Action: the Welfare State represented "the triumph of the national community over the local. It was in keeping with the trend in which central governments eliminated or sidelined the pluralistic traditions of voluntary institutions. Greater government controls and the principle of universalism brought undoubted benefits, but with the result that citizens became consumers of government rather than its producers. Paradoxically, individuals were in some ways more impotent in an age of universal suffrage and parliamentary democracy than the disenfranchised had been under an oligarchy in the past."

The outcome of representative democracy can thus be summarised as follows:

- **Poor services** that do not relate either to the individual or to the neighbourhood they live in.

- **Apathy** about representative democracy whose hard won history is fading from the collective memory.

- **Disrespect** for the politician and political parties. Their popular rating is lower than that of the used car salesman.

- **Danger**, for the credibility gap between those who represent and those who are represented is wide and widening.

This is sad, for many politicians are good, hard working and caring people. But, we must conclude that representative democracy has gone just about as far as it can go before it must make a further quantum leap in its evolution if it is again to become valued and respected. See figure 7.

Status quo = Despair

The Nature of the old Local Authority	The consequence for the neighbourhood
Budgets were administered centrally. These funded services throughout a local authority's whole territory.	Neither local people nor officers nor Councillors knew what those services cost each agency, let alone what the cost of all services was in each particular neighbourhood.
The Local Authority used to set its own budget to deliver/provide services throughout its domain with no regard to the boundaries of the neighbourhood which were contained within it.	Residents played no part at all in delivering services or assisting with the management or government of the neighbourhood. They certainly had no funds or budget of their own.
The Local Authority was concerned with the inputs it made into the whole urban area it covered. But, while it paid great attention to expenditure, tracking and administering its budgets correctly, it was not interested in the outputs, the effect of these on people in neighbourhoods.	The outputs of City funded and supplied services are registered in neighbourhoods as being consistently poor – low educational standards, high crime, etc. All people could do in response was register dismay or anger.
Councillors commanded and set policy. Officers administered it. Officers felt responsible upwards to councillors and not downwards to the neighbourhoods in which the outputs of their actions were experienced by residents.	Residents played no part at all in shaping policy, services and outputs, except for the 25 per cent of adults who vote once a year in elections. They felt powerless and excluded.
Local Authority services were one-size-fits-all monopolies. No diversity or choice was offered. The initial instinct of old style MPs, Councillors and Officers who wanted to solve the problems of Neighbourhoods of Despair, which their old-style organisation had helped to create, was to throw more money at them. This only made the inputs bigger and the outcomes worse. It wasted money. It did not solve the problem.	The only way any resident could exercise a choice for themselves was if they could muster the finances and effort to move to a 'better' neighbourhood elsewhere. The unheard, unregistered cry from the heart of residents in Neighbourhoods of Despair was: ● "Please do better than this." ● "We know what we want, but we don't know how to achieve it." ● "Give us the knowledge and resources and we will find a way." ● We are excluded from the political process.

Figure 7

Participatory Democracy

As government increased in size it came to both 'steer' and 'row' the huge ships of state, to set tasks so enormous and general that it could not carry them out efficiently. In so doing it took more and more functions and responsibilities from people and did them itself. But, in trying to both row and steer for everyone it came to do nothing very well and gained the suspicion and distrust of ordinary people who came to feel they could do far better themselves.

If people are to undertake more themselves, and take the responsibility for the quality of their lives in neighbourhoods, this frees government to concentrate on monitoring the quality of the work undertaken, disseminate best practice and find more effective ways of enabling large numbers of people at ground level to do what it once did from the top down. This could make representative democracy more understandable and acceptable. But it also entails adding the non-party political participation of people to the political process.

The greater involvement of people in the delivery of services to their neighbourhood and in the government of their lives is unlike representative democracy in a number of ways:

- It is not party-political. It entails people of all political persuasions and none joining together to associate with each other and construct their own solutions.

- Votes are held every year in representative democracy. This determines which lot are 'in' power and which lot are 'out' of it. In participatory democracy, people are not 'in' or 'out'. All who wish to be 'in' are 'in'.

- Yet, being 'in' power implies that others are 'out' of it and that the amount of power is limited. In participatory democracy it is in the interest of existing participants that they persuade more and more neighbours to become involved. Power multiplies. It grows and spreads.

All those concerned with litter can and should deal with it. All those concerned with neighbourhood-wide decisions can and should be involved. The Greek City State built an arena in which all citizens could gather and decide the issue of the day. Modern technology enables the modern community to do likewise. There is no need for elections of the kind which representative democracy requires. For, participatory democracy aims to involve all the people all of the time.

Residents in troubled neighbourhoods have become as disorganised and powerless today as were factory workers 100 years ago. Capacity Builders who recognise this and help residents associate together and organise to improve their living environment act like the shop stewards who helped to organise disorganised factory workers. Indeed, in Balsall Heath when residents took to their communal street corners to face down pimps, drug dealers and kerb crawlers, they called themselves 'pickets'. Later, they employed an organiser to identify 'good neighbours', active people who would take responsibility for each street. They called these active citizens 'street stewards' and formed an association of them to represent the interests of the whole community to the police and city authorities and to build an array of local associations through which people could do things for themselves and each other.

There are 500 residents in this association. They all meet regularly. The parallel between this form of community organisation and the way the first trade and chartist unions operated a hundred years ago is striking. Perhaps today's National Trade Unions could now join Business in the Community in helping the fractured neighbourhoods in which their members live to become more effectively organised in mutual associations. We need a Trade Union in the Community (TUitC) as well as a Business in the Community (BitC). Interestingly, Jimmy Knapp has visited Balsall Heath and applauded the application of Trade Union organising principles to life in communities. It is even more interesting to note that the co-operative movement's Unity Trust Bank, whose president is Mr Knapp, seconded one of its managers to help Balsall Heathans get a better deal from 'the system.' BitC and TUitC in partnership!

In Balsall Heath a Neighbourhood Forum is attended by two representations from each of 17 residents groups and 56 voluntary organisations. Once a year they elect an executive of 15 residents who meet on a monthly basis. The executive operates with a range of working groups which include everyone who wishes to play a part.

In Walsall, each of 19 neighbourhoods now elect a Committee of residents on a street by street basis. That is 100 or so residents elect 1 representative for a year and co-opt anyone prepared to do voluntary work to a neighbourhood committee of up to 30 strong. A host of different kinds of Neighbourhood Forums now exist in most parts of the land. As yet, few have been given the powers of those in Walsall which have a decisive say over significant parts of the budgets apportioned to their neighbourhood.

The key feature of all these Fora or Urban Village Councils is to involve as many people as possible, not to exclude these who are not 'voted in' but to include all who wish to play a part. Not unlike their rural Parish Council counterparts, Neighbourhood Fora are a new and vital part of the democratic landscape. Given the teeth, time, space and resources described earlier, they are capable of transforming the environmental, social and caring landscape of their small patch. Together, they are the basic building block of renewal on a national scale.

Capacity Builders, Entrepreneurial Managers and the new Town Hall

Although it is relatively novel to the urban scene, the active citizen's neighbourhood forum, their Capacity Builder and those local voluntary and non-government institutions which relate and are accountable to them do not comprise an additional layer of government, which further complicates the organisation of the democratic process. Rather, they take the place of significant parts of the previously over-intrusive city machine. As a consequence, the Town Hall can concentrate less on trying to run everything and thus failing to do anything well, but, like any enlightened manager, on enabling and resourcing others to achieve excellence.

Because so many of the tasks once undertaken by the Town Hall can readily and more effectively be discharged within each urban village neighbourhood it is necessary to reduce its size and change the way it is organised. Most of the Town Hall's vertically organised, top – down, departments can be slimmed down or merged in order to meet the new horizontal functions of the kind which neighbourhoods really need. Having lost the control and management of 'their' schools to school governors, a number of authorities have closed down their education committees. Kirklees has done this as has Calderdale, Rotherham, Barnsley, Gateshead, Hammersmith, Brighton, Hove, and Fulham. Once an authority has also let go of all its houses and some of its other services it will need to rethink its whole point and purpose. The local authority of tomorrow will look very different from that of today.

It follows that a fresh, community-sensitive, city department is needed which cuts horizontally across the city's old vertically designed bureaucratic and professional specialisms. This new department might subtend an array of sub-departments, one for each neighbourhood. These neighbourhood sub-departments would marshal and deploy the levers of local government to service and enhance the growth points of each neighbourhood. The old and new roles of councillors and participating good neighbours are summarised in figures 8 and 9.

Adding Participation to representation.

Existing Representative Councillors	New Participating Neighbourhood Stewards
Represent a ward of 25,000 plus people	Enable the 100 or so people in their street to participate in the process of improving their life-chances.
Arise from the ranks of a narrow band of activists within their party and can live anywhere in the town / city or elsewhere.	Are people who, regardless of political ideology, care at a personal level for their neighbours and about very local issues because they live there.
Feel they need to represent the centrally agreed views and policies of political parties.	Feel the need to represent the views and needs of their neighbours.
Believe that change can only result from centrally made decisions.	Believe that change will result from local action.
Feel that there is little that they can do when they are in opposition.	Are never in opposition and can always take action.
Stand for an admirable but institutionalised sense of civic duty and responsibility.	Stand for new personal and local communal sense of duty and responsibility.
Are concerned with inputs and the way money is spent in the whole local Authority territory.	Are concerned with outputs and the way money is spent in their neighbourhood.
Know the existing system well and feel defensive for it and for themselves when local people play their part.	Do not know the existing system well and feel the need to change it before they can participate more fully.

Figure 8

New Partners in Participation.

New Style Councillors	Neighbourhood Stewards
Do less, enable more and provide vision for a whole urban area.	Do more in their own neighbourhood.
Are not threatened by new developments, but help their old-style, top-down, departments to find new ways of working horizontally at neighbourhood level.	Respond and form good working partnerships with new style representative councillors.
Are paid as if they were professionals because they have become professional managers in charge of the devolution of huge budgets of taxpayers money and are responsible for the inspectors of outputs.	Are, like old-style Councillors, unpaid people who put in a substantial voluntary effort.
Are already recognised as competent to take decisions which not only affect neighbourhoods but whole Local Authority areas. Nonetheless, training is needed if they are to manage new style City Departments, Neighbourhood Managers and Neighbourhood Officers.	Require support and training to build their capacity to influence local events. Just as the newly forming Trades Unions movement needed to found Ruskin College and run 'workers' Education courses to enable its shop stewards to become more effective, so also street stewards who are helping people in neighbourhood to organise their affairs need a Community College.

Figure 9

These roles are not entirely new. Many towns have developed neighbourhood offices in recent years, though not always in response to a clear neighbourhood voice. The Capacity Builder and Neighbourhood Forums can provide that voice. They can be the locally accountable body to which city government devolves funds and functions.

Because the aim of this new department is to boost the confidence and capacity of the individual, see to it that others assist the developing child and take part in the revitalisation of neighbourhoods it could be called the Neighbourhood Enterprise Department. Once this new department is devolved out to area offices in each neighbourhood it, in effect, becomes their new mini or Neighbourhood Town Hall.

Its staff will be joined by officers from the police, primary care group and representatives from the private sector in the Senior Neighbourhood Managers inter-agency team. Together they will work with the Neighbourhood Forum and its staff to devise and deliver the Neighbourhood's Development Plan.

The Neighbourhood's Town Hall becomes the new Local Authority's devolved top-down lever with which other statutory agencies and the Neighbourhood Forum liaises. It might be based in an extension of one of the neighbourhood's schools or in its village hall thus becoming one of its finest and most valued local features.

Far from there being the need to worry about the 'democratic deficit' the devolution of services to neighbourhood teams and the community creates a substantial 'democratic advantage'.

The Advance of Democracy

1. Privatisation and profit or access and accountability?

Their ideological mindsets caused both the advocates and critics of public sector reforms to confuse it with the "privatisation" of the economy and the return of care from accountable politicians and bureaucrats to profit making economic entrepreneurs.

In practice, the reform of the public sector has radically different implications from that of the private sector. It creates local mutual associations and entails participatory democracy.

2. Handing control from central/local government to communities is democratic and accountable.

In place of a local education authority Education committee of 15 councillors who once managed, say, the 300 schools in its sphere of control each school is now in the charge of 15 governors. That is, in place of 15 remote councillors, these schools are now managed by 15 x 300 = 4,500 people. And, of course, parent governors are elected by parents, staff and so on.

The same point applies to tenants whose flats and homes were once managed by Council Housing Departments and which are now managed by themselves. Far more, not less, people are involved. In Balsall Heath and other neighbourhoods, where nobody previously participated in the affairs of the community, now hundreds, even thousands, do.

3. Transfer of control neither decreases nor increases costs.

A house run by a tenant, a school run by governors does not necessarily cost any less or any more than when local government managed them. The cost to the taxpayer is more or less the same. Simply, the money is managed differently. It is no longer in the hands of remote officials but the people who know how best to spend it well. Thus, it is spent more effectively. It goes further.

4. Transfer of control gives assets and pride to people in neighbourhoods.

A house or school managed by local government does not, by definition, belong to the neighbourhood in which it is based. It is thus treated by local people as if it is some remote person's responsibility. It belongs to 'them' and not 'us'. It is 'in' but not a part 'of' the community. Once it is locally owned, local people's attitude to the care and maintenance of it is transformed. Because they own and manage it they take pride in it. From being dependent on others, this makes local people independent, confident, self-reliant. Good citizenship and care for others is personalised and made real.

5. Transfer of control is not an attack on local or central government.

Simply because the state does not own or manage a house or school does not mean they no longer have a role to play in relation to them. On the contrary, as with schools standards and inspection, it is most important that both central and local government set the highest standards and inspect the quality and standard of life in neighbourhoods to ensure they are satisfactory.

Further, of course, only government can agree and allocate taxpayers funds between schools and other local neighbourhood agencies. So, it is not that either bigger or smaller government is called for, but a different kind of government whose pace and vision is not held back by confusing it with the need to supply and manage services.

6. Transfer of control means the new owners will make a profit.

There is no harm in running a social agency so well that it costs less for local people to run than the bureaucrats spent on it. However, it does not follow that the "spare" money should be given to the head teacher or senior neighbourhood manager or that it should be 'returned' to sender. Rather it should be reinvested in better plant, people, research and development.

There is currently much speculation about private sector educational business taking over failing schools. But schools are likely to be looked after as well if not better by a successful head operating on the not-for profit public sector principle whilst using best business and entrepreneurial managerial practice.

Yet, the successful head, capacity builder and neighbourhood manager will surely be more alert if they know that good results will be reflected in their salary.

A new role for the local authority.

Territorial nationalism is becoming weaker. In the European world of post industrial technology and instant communication, nationalism fades in the face of the global village. At once, power moves up and away from the borders of this country to Brussels and world-wide markets and, at the same time, it is shifting down to the urban village, street corner, family and individual.

In the new world of the new millennium the grip of the national politician and the industrially shaped political party will become even more tenuous while the role of the urban authority and the previously ordinary, inconsequential, citizen will become more and more significant.

It is in this context that the radical reform of the old-style Local Authority does not, as some supposed the Conservative government's reforms of the '80's intended, imply its abolition. Rather, it suggests the development of a highly effective new kind of local government. One of the major roles of this new authority will be to create neighbourhood-specific devolved departments. There is, however, a range of other tasks which can only be discharged from an over-arching civic centre. These include:

- The allocation of budgets between neighbourhoods, although this can be done by means of a nationally agreed, value-added, formula.

- Responsibility for the dissemination of best practice between neighbourhoods, the inspection of the performance and services of mini-Town Halls and Neighbourhood Managers and the application of sanctions if agreed targets are not met.

- Just as there is the need to close the failing school, sack the head and re-open it under new management, so there is the need to do the same with failing neighbourhoods where officers from pre-existing departmental silos fail to play as a team.

- Responsibility for transport policy.

- The oversight of refuse collection and disposal.

- Planning decisions when these impact beyond the confines of any one neighbourhood.

- The branding and marketing of their urban area to the nation, Europe and the global village.

However, there is no reason why the elected local authority councillors and their slimmed down and redrawn departments should themselves perform any of these functions. Rather, it is merely essential that they ensure that some competent body is contracted to undertake them. The councillor's role is that of the conductor of the orchestra, and not that of the many instrumentalists of the orchestra itself.

This change has already taken place in the case of Local Education Authorities where such functions as inspection, careers advice, the provision of supply teachers etc. are more competently provided by a new breed of independent educational enterprise. It is similarly to be expected that some of the functions which Local Authorities have undertaken will, in future, be discharged by:

- Neighbourhood Forums themselves or clusters of them.
- Community Development Trusts and other self-governing local agencies.
- Independent suppliers in the private sector.
- Consortia of these.

In addition to devolving many of its old functions and budgets to neighbourhood level and checking that the desired targets and outcomes are achieved, there is one crucial central function which will grow.

The old, industrial, function of towns which drew agricultural labour from the green fields to staff the urban factory's workbench has long gone. The new high-tech industries, commerce and tourism, are the means by which new economic purpose is being given to urban areas by businesses and local authorities working in partnership. If these partnerships do not blossom, some towns may never acquire a new purpose. Like the 'ghost town' of the spaghetti Western film they may die.

Regardless of Whitehall those that do flourish are likely to build upon their international connections, become more like city-states and less dependent on the nation state. As these modern towns develop new, non-industrial, functions the role of the City-Centre Manager will become more and more important. Only 10 years ago there were just 4 such managers. Now there are over 200 of these posts in 200 urban areas. Town Centre managers have turned around the faded image of their town or city centre into a vibrant one with the help of private and public sector initiatives.

There is much interesting talk of rediscovering a national identity and of re-branding Britain. But the need to perform this service for towns and cities is of paramount importance if they are to develop a new post-industrial role. Neither the private nor public sector alone can achieve this. Imaginative new initiatives are called for and many exciting examples are now to be found in different urban areas which owe nothing to the politics of the past and everything to Councillors and City Officers who have helped their town or city to find a new purpose and pride. Birmingham's image was of metal bashing and Spaghetti junction. Today, it is of canals, the International Convention Centre, the NEC, and a World Class Symphony Orchestra. It is twinned not with London but with major European Cities. It has offices in Brussels and Chicago. And, at home, it has meetings with Bristol, Manchester, Sheffield and Nottingham in an alliance which could come to overshadow the importance of the one it has with the capital.

The newly emerging role of the Local Authority and the neighbourhood is summarised in figure 10.

New Style **popularly elected executive managers** or Mayors of towns and cities will soon be common place. Preferably they will not be fading party political people selected by the usual political process, but independent minded characters who will put the real, non theatrical, needs of their urban area first.

Radical reform = Hope

Authority	Neighbourhood
Does less itself and enables people in neighbourhoods to do more.	Stops grumbling that the Authority isn't solving its problem and takes local action to solve them.
Changes its political and planning lines to coincide with these of socially/ geographically defined neighbourhoods.	Builds a neighbourhood spirit, identifies and 'beets their bounds'.
Appoints a Civic Entrepreneur as a Neighbourhood Manager with a small team of interdependent officers whose task is to target inputs so as to achieve outputs agreed with the community.	Appoints a Social Entrepreneur or Forum officer whose tasks is to help local people to form new local associations and a neighbourhood Forum.
Negotiates the cost of all the neighbourhood Development Plans in its area, divides and devolves its budget between these neighbourhoods.	Draws up a Neighbourhood Development Plan and costs it.
Commissions each neighbourhood to deliver its plan.	Implements its plan and reviews it year on year. Implementation includes each neighbourhood in: ● Providing some services itself. ● Buying in others from elsewhere e.g. other neighbourhoods, and the private sector as well as the Local Authority.
Agrees a set of standards to be achieved in each neighbourhood, then inspects to ensure the agree targets/outputs are met.	Revises targets in line with inspections of its outputs.
The local Authority gains respect and the satisfaction of its customers.	The neighbourhood gains choice, diversity and the services and outputs it wants and the sense of: ● Responsibility ● Inclusion ● Pride
A number of functions remain. These include services which only the Local Authority can accept responsibility for and deliver or commission because they affect all neighbourhoods. Examples include: ● Developing and marketing a vision for the town/city centre and for the town/ city as a whole. ● Transportation policy. ● Inspection of the quality of services in neighbourhoods. ● Representation to government. ● Representation to Europe and other towns and cities.	Neighbourhoods are the basic building blocks from which the wider City 'neighbourhood of neighbourhoods' is built. They form an active, two way, relationship with it.

Figure 10

They will govern with the help of a **Cabinet of Senior Councillors** who will champion new departments ranging from the one which markets their urban area nationally and internationally and that which empowers and enables the many neighbourhoods within its boundaries to find their identities and deliver their own self-help services.

Just in case anyone supposes that the 'remaining' democratically elected Councillors are being demoted and will have little to do, the very opposite is the case. Each neighbourhood will need an elected representative champion who will present the needs of its participatory Forum, Senior Manager and Trust to the Mayor and Cabinet. Hitherto, local Councillors have been the very opposite of local. Once elected, they have disappeared into the corridors of power in the Town Hall and have had no visible local effect other than to become the back-bench voting fodder of their party's kitchen cabinets. In future, it will be important for them to become a respected local figure who is applauded for gaining the resources their neighbourhood needs to build its capacity and deliver its neighbourhood plan. This will, of course, entail redrawing local political boundaries so that they coincide with social neighbourhood ones. Again, the changes entailed are considerable and will take several years to achieve.

The great Victorian Town Halls which symbolised municipal splendour at home while Britain's Empire expanded abroad have become decaying monuments to a past era. Yet, while cotton mills and docks have been closed and reopened as offices and museums and business has adopted a new style of devolved organisation, the multi-million pound organisations of local government still hanker for past security and are often an impediment to growth. If more of them do not also move with the times and find a fresh way of catching the voters' imagination their future will be in doubt and the worrying credibility gap which the opening paragraphs of this chapter described will continue to widen.

So, although the reforms proposed are radical and require dramatic changes in style, attitude and outcome, they represent no more of an attack upon local government or the Welfare State than John Harvey Jones' attempts to save fading industrial businesses by importing information technology and rethinking the way they are managed signify an attack upon them. On the contrary, the reforms could rescue the political process from decades of inertia and popular resentment and herald a new era of acceptance, appreciation and vigorous growth.

Chapter 8:

A Rolling Programme of Renewal

While local, bottom-up essays in renewal have been battling against the top-down tide for many years, we are now in the early days of a major national programme of renewal. This programme begins with the assumption that, however well meaning, all previous top-down attempts at regeneration have been flawed because:

- They tried to do things 'for' people and not 'with' them.
- They were of time-limited duration.
- They left mainstream budgets intact and did not change attitudes.
- They tackled only a few of the 3,000 troubled neighbourhoods in need of regeneration.
- They did not change the culture. They merely rearranged the deckchairs while the Titanic sailed on regardless.
- They did not engage with and were not driven by the bottom-up.
- They wasted money and created resentment.

In order to guarantee success this time a limited number of successful pilots are needed which chart the way for others to follow. After the model building of the early years, in each subsequent year 200 plus new neighbourhoods must become involved until the ambitious national target of 3,000 plus is met in the year 2015 plus.

To picture adequately the vision and effort which is required, it is useful to think back to the point in the 80's when the government of the day first experimented with the Local Management of schools in Cambridgeshire. Could successful pilots be formed? Could LEAs be forced to hand over some of their budgets and control to all schools? Could all schools one day become self-governing? Could each school be run not by the LEA but by its Head and Board of Governors drawn from the community?

At first, only some schools received part of their budget and old attitudes died hard. A decade later, all schools have 90% of their budget and are, in effect, self-governing. Attitudes have changed and services once provided by the LEA are provided by schools themselves and new educational enterprises. LEAs have changed out of sight and, in some instances, have merged with other departments as their Empire ended and they found a new role. Over time, it will be the same with Local Authorities generally as more and more neighbourhoods come to practice Neighbourhood Management in more and more of their neighbourhoods.

Perhaps it can now be seen that this strategy for the empowerment of people and a renaissance in the nation's urban areas is not some new form of Urban Aid or SRB to be tried for 2 or 3 years and then left. The new approach defines urban regeneration not as a programme to be funded for a few years by central government but as an on-going process, a new way of managing the way we care for each other in communities and spend the nation's welfare budget. Good Neighbourhood Management is urban renewal. It puts the Welfare Society in the place of the Welfare State.

A national centre for renewal

A great deal, but not enough, is now known about good regeneration practice. The social capital created by the first Capacity Builders and Civic Entrepreneurs has been documented. The Universities, Think Tanks like DEMOS and the IEA, The Joseph Rowntree Foundation, BitC and others have produced a growing library which documents much of what has been and is being done. We are embarking on a major national and local programme which reflects on and uses this existing experience and which will create new experiences which will require further reflection.

When Christopher Columbus first set sail to the West some wondered whether he would presently fall off the flat earth. He and fellow explorers not only helped to demonstrate that the earth was round by landing on American soil, they created the need for Cartographers and Geographers to chart the way for other less bold souls to follow. A whole new subject and profession resulted which made it easier and less demanding for the next generation of sailors. The unknown journey which marks the route from troubled neighbourhoods to vibrant ones is now being similarly charted and the best ways of helping people to associate together are being spelled out. Presently, the task of the Capacity Builder and Senior Neighbourhood Manager will become rather more straight forward and uncontroversial.

The new professions of Capacity Builder and Neighbourhood Management are arising people before our eyes. Soon, hundreds and thousands of these people will be needed to staff the 3000 neighbourhoods in need of support, let alone most other neighbourhoods which may choose a less intensive form of local management.

Residents, officers, councillors and MPs will all need to know more about Neighbourhood Management. Many will benefit not just from hands-on experience but from courses, lectures, literature and DIY Toolkits. Much training and support will be needed so that we need not rely on one Christopher Columbus. Presently the social Atlantic will be crossed every day by many people.

A National Centre for Renewal is being set up. It will document and disseminate best practice. It will represent an important step forward in legitimising and making more straight forward the findings of the first social explorers and it will hold up a reflective mirror to the unfurling national programme.

Another pioneering analogy is called for. In the early days of the Trades Union movement, the shop stewards who first strode the factory floor benefited enormously from their Workers Education Association and the founding of Ruskin College. How could these ordinary and humble folk learn to be more effective in their attempts to gain better working conditions for their fellows and organise the shop floor? How could they benefit from their more experienced peers? The WEA and Ruskin college were the answer.

Today's equivalent for the resident who must be in the lead of transforming the nation's most difficult areas are Regional Residents' Centres staffed by those who have already begun the process in their own back yard.

These 'Residents for Regeneration' Centres, say, at first 4, one in the North East, one in the North West, one in the Midlands and one in the South should be based in neighbourhoods which are already on the way to recovery. They should be staffed by residents who still spend most of their time hard at work in their own neighbourhood. But, for 1 or 2 days a week they might, if requested by them to do so, visit residents who are just setting sail on the voyage of recovery elsewhere.

For some, one visit might suffice to learn about the navigational 'dos and don'ts'. For others, an on-going relationship might last for a year or more. Each ship needs its pilot.

Each Regional Centre might be able to sustain relations with 100 other neighbourhoods and introduce them to each other. Networks of good practice as well as friendships will arise. Soon, new groups of residents will be able to undertake the pioneering role of the first centres. The eventual aim might be that each urban area has its own focal point for regeneration, its own Academy of Renewal. Recall that within 15 years each urban authority will contain, on average, 20 plus Neighbourhood Management areas. Walsall aims to ensure that all its 57 neighbourhoods are managed in this way. It could be that every urban authority will eventually introduce Neighbourhood Management in each and every one of its neighbourhoods. Success will demand that they are all sustained by their own home-grown Academy of Renewal.

These Residents for Renewal Centres or Academies will not rival the National Centre. Rather they will complement it and form ladders to it from the regions and visa versa. The cost of the centres? Perhaps a few thousand of Central Government money for the first ones. But, surely, if they proved to be worth it, each neighbourhood's regeneration funds would pay for them by reimbursing the costs of their travel and time. That is, they should pay for themselves.

An inspectorate of neighbourhoods, an Offhood.

In addition to driving the renewal process forward via a national plan, local action in neighbourhoods, disseminating and supporting best practice via

National and Local centres an inspectorate of neighbourhoods, an Ofhood, is also needed.

Of course, there is already an Inspectorate of Schools, Social Services, an Audit Commission and so on. Thus, some of the necessary work is already underway. But it is not collated in each neighbourhood. While each school has been inspected nobody has put together the results of these inspections in a neighbourhood context. How, collectively, do the 6 or so schools in a neighbourhood compare, contrast and play to each other's strength? The implication is that the schools in each of the nation's 3,000 troubled communities needs an EAZ and that each EAZ as well as each school needs to be evaluated.

In addition to looking at a neighbourhood's composite educational performance an Offhood might look at the following:

- The neighbourhood's image. Is it good, bad or improving?

- The levels of crime and unemployment and whether they are changing.

- The appearance of the neighbourhood, whether its boundary is clearly defined and coincides with planning and political lines.

- The quality of Capacity Building and whether Neighbourhood Management is in place and succeeding in its task of improving and devolving services.

- Are the Local Authority, Health Authority and Police taking Neighbourhood Management seriously, disassembling budgets and resolving them at local level?

- Depending on their size have these statutory agencies reached their target of creating, say, 20 Neighbourhood Management initiatives? How many of these are succeeding? Do any need to be put under new, independent, management?

Each local partnership of bottom-up capacity builder and top-down manager may well perform much of Ofhood's task through self-evaluation and quality control. This, after all, is called for by the annual task of receiving the Neighbourhood Development Plan, updating it and setting new targets.

The main role of a national Ofhood, therefore, might be to liaise between the National and local Regeneration centres and spread good practice. It may be that it need only be called in locally when residents have failed to gain satisfactory progress from the powers that be.

The way forward

A succession of milestones mark what must be done if the ambitious national strategy is to be delivered by the year 2015. They include the need to:

- Spell out the goal of the proposed structure and culture change in clear, simple, and practical terms so that everyone knows where they are going.

- Spell out what a typical Neighbourhood Forum will look like.

- Detail the role of the Capacity Builder and Senior Neighbourhood Manager.

- Offer person specifications and likely sources of recruitment for Capacity Builders and Civil Entrepreneurs.

- Indicate just how the Neighbourhood Trust, Forum, Capacity Builder and Senior Neighbourhood Officer might relate to each other.

- Explain to all concerned why local people find it so difficult to help themselves and require time and support before they can do so.

- Provide training and support for councillors and professionals.

- State very clearly that a rolling programme of reform is required which will start with areas of best practice and will eventually encompass all inner and outer city neighbourhoods in all authority areas.

- Set up National and Regional Centres.

- Set up an Offhood.

- As with LM, Neighbourhood Management (NM) must require each Local Authority to move from A to B within "x" years.

- Provide a monitoring and mentoring service for Local Authorities.

- As with LEA's and schools, it will be vital to get tough with Local Authorities and neighbourhoods which fail, as some surely will, and offer prizes and incentives for those who succeed.

- Spell out the different scenarios (models A, B and C) which different stages of Neighbourhood Management might take.

In particular spell out:

- What should be left centrally (after 1, 2 and 3 years) other than an inspectorial, advisory and a trouble-shooting role for the most difficult neighbourhoods.

- What might be undertaken by the local, devolved, statutory team led by the senior neighbourhood manager (after 1, 2 and 3 years).

- What neighbourhood associations and community Forums might undertake (after 1, 2 and 3 years).

- What all these together might look like in models A, B and C after years 1, 2 and 3.

This list of items is coherent and mutually reinforcing. It is substantial and it will be difficulty to persuade all concerned – residents, officers and politicians at every level – to take part with enthusiasm and not damn it with faint praise.

Guidance, a clearly defined rolling programme, combined with a firm declaration by HMG that the resourcing of Capacity Building, Neighbourhood Management, the welding of participatory to representative democracy and associated attitude changes will happen should make the transition from a failed system of services to an effective one less painful and more acceptable to those who staff the existing system. Nobody should be in any doubt, however, that it will require the same degree of exhortation and prescription as has been necessary to transform the nation's schools.

It follows that whoever is appointed to the new national role of Inspector of Neighbourhoods is likely to attract just as much heat as has the Chief Inspector of Schools. At first, those who live in the nation's troubled areas will respond, while Local Authority might be anxious.

We are only at the very first stage of all of these developments. The first pilots are just vying for a place. A 15 if not a 30 year period of development lies ahead before we will be able to judge whether the nation's most difficult neighbourhoods can be included in the mainstream of life and the advantages and the positive repercussions of Neighbourhood Management will be proven.

There is all to play for. The success of LM and the virtues of a tough Ofsted Inspectorate determined to raise standards regardless of criticism from the conservative forces of the teacher's unions and the educational establishment holds out the possibility of the transformation of urban despair into hope. But success is not guaranteed.

So, just as each Neighbourhood's Development Plan needs revisiting and revising in the light of experience every year, so the National Strategy for Neighbourhood Renewal and the implementation of Neighbourhood Management in each of the nations 3,000 troubled neighbourhoods will need reviewing every year. Are we on target locally and nationally? If not, what can be done to make sure we accelerate the pace of progress?

The National and Regional Centres for Regeneration and the proposed Offhood Inspectorate will help to answer these questions with annual State of Regeneration reports.

These will, no doubt, address the values and morality, the quality, point and purpose of caring for each other. Otherwise all might fall apart and the next fleet of Columbuses might lose their way.

Chapter 9:

Revaluing society

The one remaining ingredient which completes the recipe by which life in urban neighbourhoods can be regenerated is a set of values capable of giving people a common moral purpose and enthusiasm. Common values glue people in society together through mutual trust and regard.

Such values are in scarce supply today. For, since the Enlightenment, the subjective quality of morality and the traditions which enshrined it and which were taught from generation to generation have been gradually relegated to the periphery of society. In place of a moral code, the family, church, and the priest an objective, rational, value-neutral, bureaucratic order has arisen. In the twentieth century's top-down pyramid-like command society people have become bound together not by values but by apparently rational rules and the regulations of the state.

If in future, however, the state is to do and regulate less and people are again to undertake responsibilities in more and more aspects of life, then they will need to discover a common set of values to give meaning to the associations they form and a way of upholding and teaching them which will help each generation to acquire and develop them anew.

From the beginning of social time, key people within any community have provided the moral glue which has enabled families and the wider community to stick together. Authoritative people have sustained and transmitted the values and sentiments of communal life. They were called the priest or the elders of the tribe, grand parents and so on. Where are today's equivalents of these good people and their moral motivation to be found?

It is not possible to rewind history and return to the pre-industrial world in which the extended family, the parish priest and religious values provided the warp and weft of a sturdy communal life – nor is it desirable to try. Yet, we urgently need to find acceptable modern equivalents if communal life is to become rich enough in social capital to enable people to live happy and fulfilled lives.

The question, therefore, is not whether or not to improve the quality of communal life, but how to do so. How can the qualities of moral worth, responsibility, judgement and choice be placed at the centre of the modern stage? How can we call for good people to step forward and lead a communal renaissance?

This, in part, is the distinction and challenge of the Third Way. If the state is to do less in a new age in which all have the information and confidence their 'leaders' once had, if we are all to do more and exercise responsibilities and obligations as well as rights, then what we all do in our daily lives becomes a crucial feature in the creation of the good society. It is not the case that the state, politics, and policies have ceased to be important, but that their overwhelming significance alters to make space for and respond to an empowered and morally concerned people.

We are forced to wonder with the late Cardinal Basil Hume: "Whether we are now becoming more aware that what makes for a truly good society in the end is not just better policies, but better people". And that, he added, was a "tougher challenge than the politics to which we have been accustomed." The signs are promising.

Sources of moral courage

Princess Diana's death unleashed an unprecedented outpouring of grief. The whole nation surprised itself by discovering an unpolished emotional caring and charitable characteristic which some had thought had been consigned to history. There is a moral impulse in everyone. It comes with childhood, parenthood and family life. It is the matter-of-fact, basic, foundation upon which all social life is built. If praised and encouraged rather than denigrated, it will flourish and infuse all aspects of social life. There are a range of ways by which our moral concern can be honed and practised.

1. Now that local schools have a clearer view of what each one costs and have more control over their affairs, parents and other local governors are needed to manage them. That is, people who once took the provision of the school for granted and left it to others now have to give up time and make a special effort to help it to improve. Tenants who once grumbled at the Town Hall's poor administration of their estate now sit on their estate's Board of Management. They can no longer afford to put down the litter that they once expected the Town Hall to pick up, for they now have to pick it up themselves.

2. The sheer moral courage required of those people who play an active part in their local Neighbourhood Watch or Street Watch group and reclaim their street from the thief is becoming less unique. Facing hardened, aggressive, criminals rather than turning a blind eye, forming positive relations with the unpopular police, giving up large portions of leisure time demands real effort and moral distinction. There are now over 100,000 neighbourhood watch schemes.

3. A host of ordinary people now manage and staff little local voluntary associations and community enterprises. Capacity Builders and Civic entrepreneurs work with good neighbours, help them to raise their sights, identify their skills and build their capacity to play a positive role in transforming and sustaining their confident new community.

4. Faith establishments may wish to reach further beyond their other worldly concerns and apply their enduring values to helping ordinary people to build secular associations in the domain of home, street and community. The Church of England published 'Faith in the City' in the '80s. Catholics, Methodists, Jews, Hindus and Muslims also need to find more ways of applying the principles of their faith at neighbourhood level – seven days a week, not one. They need to join with ordinary folk in making Capacity Builders of us all.

   Just as the failing business, school and neighbourhood need a development plan and enlightened leadership to transform them into a successful enterprise, so the faith establishments need to consider how the services they provide can become more appropriate to the needs of the neighbourhood in which they are based. Is the way the priest of today is recruited and trained relevant to the morally challenging task of urban regeneration? Are their buildings and resources used to maximum effect? Are the different faiths able to play to each other's strengths? Can the values of the East, which newcomers have brought from the Indian Subcontinent, meet and revive those of the West?

5. Even a better managed religious communal input is not sufficient. It is important that the DfEE now understands that schools must teach not just English, Maths and the academic subjects but 'civics', the way we live in society and value each other. Of course, the good schools teach this in the way that they are organised. 'Civics' is taught in the playground, in the corridor and at dinner time as well as in the classroom. Indeed, the best school is run as a moral community with a code of conduct which the student will take into adult life.

6. The problem which faces us, however, is so great that the teaching and practising of 'civics' to the next generation can't be left to either church or school. Following Howard Gardener, Daniel Goleman showed us that we all possess 'emotional, social and moral' intelligence as well as the academic and technical kind. Too often we forget this and leave it to chance that each individual's emotional, social and moral intelligence will become well developed. It won't. Helping these qualities of goodness towards self and others to arise in each individual requires just as much skill and dedication as does the mentoring of the musician and physician.

7. In recent times the private sector has understood that running a business does not just depend on a sharp economic mind. It entails the ability to manage people well, to provide them with good working conditions, to respect and train their skills and act on their ideas. There are now University courses and advanced degrees in 'management' for the private sector. It has benefited enormously.

   We must manage, teach and practice emotional intelligence in the family, through the 'child's rites of passage', in the way housing estate is run as well as in the school and what is left of the church.

Johnathon Sacks has pointed out the significance of the verse from Isiah: "All your children shall be students of the Lord, and great shall be the peace of your children. The Rabbis added the comment "call them not 'your children' but 'your builders'". When children became the builders of civic life, because all the associations through which they learn have taught them well, freedom is in safe hands. But, when the hands responsible for that teaching shake, freedom and peace is at risk.

As the old African saying has it: "It takes a whole village to raise a child." It takes such a child raised in such a way to sustain that society into the future. Each family, school, church, community, town and the nation will need to find ways of celebrating and acknowledging this fact. The first decades of the new millennium could mark a significant moment when ongoing celebrations could focus our attention upon the flickering candlelight of value, shield and enable it to burn brightly.

The Politics of conflict or of cohesion

While we seek common values and mutual understanding to build a cohesive society, the theories which politicians have devised to explain how society works and can be changed have viewed things from the partial perspective of just the one part of society with which they identify. When such incomplete theories have been used to guide political action they have usually clashed with other theories shaped from other perspectives. Instead of the intended progress, the outcome has been division and discord.

Just as when parents in a once loving family fall out, shout at each other, yet fail to hear what each other says, call in their legal representatives and bitterly divide what once was whole, so also people easily form opposed political camps. These have their own distinct theory of who is to blame and how things can be put right if only every one else accepts their own partial way of seeing things.

It is difficult for a family in strife to care well for each of its members. Responsibilities and obligations once instinctively and freely, even joyfully, given become calculated and unfeeling. Resentment comes to the fore. All are the poorer and the family is rendered impotent. The same is true of society. It is far less easy for anyone to consider the welfare of all the members of a whole society when it is divided. Resentments and selfish rights get too easily in the way of obligations. Contending parties look at each other's faults rather than play to each other's strengths. The social and financial costs mount.

The Conservative Party has been associated with the private sector and the more affluent, while Labour grew from the Trades Unions and is linked to the needy. The former advocates economic individualism, fewer taxes, smaller government. The latter advocates social and economic collectivism, larger taxes and bigger government. Regardless of our own sympathies, we have to accept that both of these theories are partial and unable on their own to reflect how society as a whole functions. They relate more to the sectional and self-concerned interests of one part of society. In practice, these different theories hinder the development of an integrated overview. This has been the story of the last century of the past millennium.

There is a brighter possibility. Just as the once unhappy family can find harmony because the partners are persuaded to see things from each other's point of view, so also social conflict can be healed when the partial truths of warring parties are put together into a mutually acceptable consensus which can unite and motivate everyone. In so doing, each must abandon cherished assumptions, come to see things differently and contribute to a socially productive outcome. In place of the Conservative's first and Labour's second way, this is the politics and theory of the third way. But each and every party may adopt it. Indeed, it is part of a wider non-party political social perspective which is concerned with boosting society as a whole and not one section of it.

At the beginning of the twentieth century Sigmond Freud wrote 'The Psychopathology of Everyday Life' in which he showed how people could grow up to become personally and socially crippled because of troubled relations in their early years with their parents. At the end of the century Mihali Csikszentmihalyi wrote 'Living well: The Psychology of everyday life'. He explains in it how harmonious relations at home can set the child on course to becoming a well adjusted and dynamic individual. He shows that when the individual is alert, body and mind well practised and operating as one, they have clear aims and know how to achieve them, then they can experience 'flow'. The concert pianist or athlete feel this 'flow' when at the peak of their power. So can a team, as when the French football team beat the Brazilians in the '98 World Cup final. Man for man a less talented side, they combined together with a zest and spirit which gave them added value.

Csikszentmihalyi shows that from time to time not just a person or a team, a school or business, but a whole society can become so balanced and in tune that it can experience social 'flow'.

More recently the author dared to take his tax paying business friend, who had been so outraged while being asked to help an outer area, to Balsall Heath in inner city Birmingham where people have done much to rebuild their shattered community with little outside help.

"This is more like it," he declared. "I can see that any pound I give, they'll multiply and make use of. I'll second one of my best managers to you, give you office space and bring some of my colleagues in other businesses to have a look. Maybe they can help as well." He said: "This is not charity. Every high street needs a thriving back street if it is to succeed." He saw a productive relationship between the private and public which, in other times, he might have opposed."

Closing down the old way of managing and funding troubled neighbourhoods and opening them up under new management to create neighbourhoods which experience 'flow' is important for three reasons:

- It is good for taxpayers, who want to see their money used productively.

- It is good for recipients, who want to gain the pride which comes from realising hope.

- It is good for both donors and recipients, whose relationship was institutionalised by the state and turned into antagonism by the political parties. Donor and recipient can be brought together. Social division can be replaced by the common sense of responsibility and the moral society.

In place of the division which the Welfare State had inadvertently injected into the relationship between those who have much and those who have little, the Welfare Society which is emerging in our inner and outer city areas is founded on mutual understanding, harmony and 'flow'. This balanced relationship is infinitely more socially productive and satisfying than one based on the political conflict of opposed classes.

Once known, long-forgotten, Lessons from the 1800's

Members of the Labour Party who feel their existing vocabulary of class and conflict and equality does not yet match the growth points of the freshly emerging, morally driven, relations between the private, public and third sectors may find some comfort in looking farther back in history than the collectivism which has dominated the twentieth century.

The Chartists and Co-operators practised ethical socialism in the 1800's and built the first Trades Unions. Robert Owen didn't try to take control of the state to legislate for schools for all. He built schools with and for those who attended his factories. In those days, ethical socialists didn't wait for others to do things for them. They created an astonishing array of thriving local associations which gave meaning and value to their families and neighbours. This was not an uncaring or selfish individualism. It was both individual and human-scale neighbourly mutual care at the same time.

Friendly societies arose later in the nineteenth century. Working people contributed gladly to them knowing that those who fell upon hard times would be helped. They employed their own administrators and doctors. By the end of that century 7,000,000 people belonged to a friendly society.

In those nineteenth century days, it would have been difficult to predict that the twentieth century would see the rise of the Welfare State. For, many people envisaged that the Friendly Societies and Mutual Associations would develop their role of providing assistance for people who became sick or unemployed or old. Powerful arguments were, therefore, developed in those days to show that 'progress' would consist in increased wages for working people so that they could contribute more of their earnings to their Friendly Society so that it could provide a greater range of Welfare Services.

In Friendly Societies, rights and responsibilities were intertwined and freely given. People supported each other. If the state was allowed to take on this function then, it was supposed, ordinary people would have to demonstrate their right to support it. Thus, it would no longer be necessary for people to exercise responsibility. The state would do it for them and this, people thought, was wrong and diminishing. Rights and responsibilities would become separated and opposed to each other. The quality of life would suffer. Déjà vu!

In addition to the prophets, the chartists, co-operators and mutualists have all taught us that people are individuals. Yet, they can only express their individuality and become fully human in a family, collective, communal and moral setting. Individualism and collectivism are not, as the political parties would have us believe, incompatible opposites, they are essential flip sides of the same human coin. At different times in history, however, one side of this coin has been emphasised by philosophers and politicians to the detriment of the other. This has resulted in discordant social relations, a divided and uneasy society.

The development of an approach which combines the virtues of both collectivist and individualistic ways of organising social affairs could mark the end of a period of major debate and conflict between those who argued for a caring public state and those who have advocated private initiative.

The diagrams in figure 11 shows that there are a number of different ways of picturing relationships between the three enduring features of society – the economic or private sector, the public sector of central and local government, and family and communal life, the third sector. Different combinations of these three sectors have existed at different times in the last 200 years. Some of these combinations have been more effective than others.

Diagram 1 shows that in the 1800's the public sector was relatively small. It looked after foreign policy but it had only begun the task of thinking about its role in relationship to law, order and domestic policy. The private sector was largely a law unto itself as the industrial revolution developed into full swing and expanded into the emergent Empire.

The communal, third, sector looked after the home, neighbours and spiritual life through a variety of self sustaining associations. The three sectors – public, private and community were distinct. But their significance and relationship with each other was about to change dramatically.

The public sector gradually expanded to take on many of the functions of the community sector which, as a consequence, became weak leaving individuals dependent on public provision. The public sector intruded into and nationalised 'the commanding heights' of the public sector. Diagram 2 illustrates the pyramid-like, top-down, outcome of this. Enterprise, individuality and self-reliance diminished. Society became sluggish and unwieldy. This epitomises the second, socialist, way.

Margaret Thatcher and Keith Joseph stand for the first way. Their vision was not so much to return to the last century as to release first the private and then the communal sector from the dead hand of top-down central planning. They

Models of the relationship between the public, private and community sector.

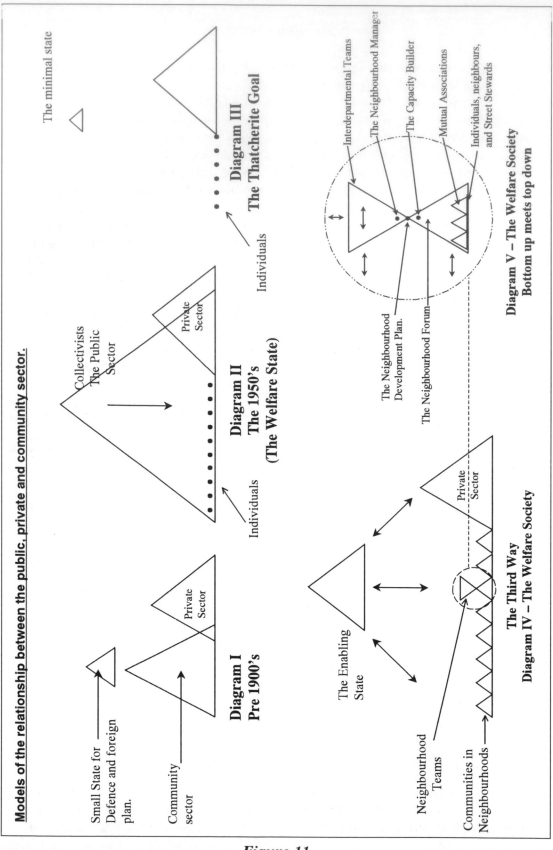

Figure 11

aimed to privatise both. But, in doing so, they had to argue that there was 'no such thing as society,' only the individual.

In seeking to roll back the frontiers of the public sector, they pictured the laissez faire situation in which the individual, whether at work or at home was just that, an individual and not a part of a wider, communal, whole.

Diagrams 4 and 5 show what can happen if we combine the virtues of the first and second way and build a modern version of the balance between public, private and communal sectors which existed before the extension of the public sector.

In constructing a strong and distinct communal sector with the help of Capacity Builders and Civic Entrepreneurs and a vibrant set of common values we are not 'privatising' the local associations through which people live. Rather, we are returning them to the co-operative and mutual relationships by which people naturally support each other.

For this to happen, the public sector must stop both steering and rowing. Instead, it is required to concentrate on enabling others, whether in the private or communal sectors, to respectively generate economic and social capital.

We stand at the dawn of a new era. In place of the public control and uniformity of the industrial era and the Welfare State we are about to experience:

■ A renaissance of communal enterprise, self-help and the building of substantial social capital.

■ A remodelling of the public sector so that it enables and does not provide or diminish.

Indeed, as post-industrial society emerges from the cocoon of constraint, we can now accept that it has for too long been supposed that only the well-educated few, an elite 20 per cent of the population, the confident, ambitious and affluent are competent to run their own independent institutions, look after their own houses, use private health care and private schools and run their own businesses. Similarly, for too long, it has been assumed that the less educated 80 per cent and the excluded 30 per cent of the population were so incompetent and dependent that they could only be housed, made healthy and educated by the educated elite within one-size-fits-all institutions which the re-distribution State provided. The belief that most people can do none of the things which the affluent can achieve and that to dream of doing so should be positively discouraged has prevailed only because it has been assumed that people or, rather most people, do not make society but are made by it.

A movement to renew the social environment.

In place of strife and political discord, something of a non – and all party and all-faith movement is emerging. After arising as a fringe concern, followed by a long period of both national and local discussion, most people now accept that the natural ecology of the earth cannot indefinitely absorb the post enlightenment outputs of unrestrained scientific and industrial progress – excavations, emissions, pollution and toxic wastes – without serious damage being done to the land, sea and air. The environmentalists have shown us over the last 30 years that without links being made between personal responsibility and the common good the planet will be destroyed. Therefore, we are all beginning to apply the principles of stewardship to the natural environment so as to conserve it for the benefit of future generations. We all now worry about and seek to repair the hole in the ozone layer.

The same principles are now being applied to the social terrain. It is becoming increasingly clear that the foundations and guiding axioms of social and cultural life also do not have an infinite capacity to withstand the erosion which results from 'taking out more than is put back in.' As with the earth, social life in developed countries like modern Britain has also been ravaged to such an extent by the age of industry, its organisation structures and concepts, that it has become impossible to maintain a civilised life in key parts of the nation. So, the task of each succeeding generation must now be to steward society and leave the quality of social and cultural life as well as the natural environment in a better condition than when they found it.

In times past, change was so slow that the torn fabric of the community would be refurbished without many people having to think or act overtly about it. It just happened with the helping hand of grand-parent, doctor, priest and squire. Today, it will not. As a whole nation we all now need to consciously invest time and resources to discover and apply the best means of replenishing and sustaining community at the levels of family and local neighbourhood as well as in the wider society.

As with environmental stewards, the work of Capacity Builders and Civic Entrepreneurs was at first isolated and unrecognised. They swam against the tide. They did not figure on the agenda of politicians. Now, a sea change is taking place. The unravelling of communal associations has become so marked and the consequences are so shockingly apparent in troubled neighbourhoods that the whole nation has become alarmed. The 'hole in the social ozone layer' is now as worrying to people, if not more so, than the physical hole in the atmosphere.

This sea change in appreciation and attitude presents Capacity Builders leading political, religious and other reformers with a major opportunity.

As it has taken 50 years since the Second World War to build the Welfare State and 200 years for the Enlightenment to inadvertently erode thousands of years of accumulated tradition, it is unlikely that the task of reconstruction can be achieved by any one party or overnight.

What better time to start this huge task of driving an urban renaissance, of reinventing and invigorating the way we relate to each other than as, at the cusp of time, we set sail in the adventurous, uncharted, waters of a new millennium. What better way of depicting the task than to say it entails moving from the style and nature of a Welfare State to those of a Welfare Society – see figure 12.

The Welfare State	The Welfare Society
• Poverty is the result of physical deprivation.	• Poverty is the result of the lack of individual and communal skills, capacity and vision.
• Poverty can be solved by the Top down reallocation of income. The receipt of income supplement is a right.	• Poverty can be solved by helping people to develop skills, the sense of self help and personal responsibility.
• Poor people and neighbourhoods can be helped by supply side planning and "one size fits all" services.	• Poor people and neighbourhoods can only be helped if services are customised and as far as possible owned and managed by the "recipients".
• Large centralised departments deliver services vertically regardless of the common sense of community.	• Delivery needs, as far as possible, to relate to identifiable neighbourhoods and to be customised.
• Education is to be delivered through comprehensive schools to children between the ages of 5 and 16.	• Education is life long and must be customised.
• Health is a matter for Hospitals and G.P.s.	• Health is also a matter for the individual and local community.
• Community Safety is a matter for the police.	• Community Safety crucially involves residents in partnership with the Police.
• Representative democracy enables MPs and Councillors, central and Local Government to legislate to solve poverty.	• Participatory Democracy must be added to a reformed Representative Democracy so that a new compact between people and the state can solve poverty.
• There is a fixed amount of power available to society.	• Power can grow. People do not have to take it from others in order to acquire it.
• The Welfare State and its services are value neutral and non-judgemental.	• The welfare Society is bound together by Values and thus makes moral judgements.

Figure 12

Chapter 10:

Conclusion

Creating the Welfare Society, and precipitating an Urban Renaissance does not just entail radical changes in unemployment benefits which encourage people back to work, or pensions, which encourage people not to rely on the state but on their own savings. The necessary reforms must encompass schools, houses, health, safety and the environment over which the state had assumed ownership and control. In all of these aspects of life it is now clear that the individual, families and neighbours must play a more active and responsible role. They must take back from the state the ownership and control of the quality and style of the caring services if the individual is to become a proud and included part of the mainstream of society.

Many of these reforms focus on the need to manage services, the way we care for each other, in ways which are quite unlike those which have prevailed for the whole of the twentieth century. The proposed reforms cluster around the new professional roles of Capacity Building and Neighbourhood Management.

The new National Centre for Urban Renewal needs the support of a series of complementary resident-led regional ones to train more and more people to undertake these demanding roles. For the first time, a way of inspecting neighbourhoods and holding those who deliver services in them to account is called for. To redress persistent failure in the most troubled 3,000 areas it is necessary to create an entirely different type of management for them and vest ownership within each neighbourhood.

Taken together, these reforms comprise a major change in the way society is organised. The post war consensus held that Representative Democracy, higher taxation, the redistribution of wealth and the top down provision by the State of personal social security, houses, schools, safety and so on would create a fairer, more equal and inclusive society at ease with itself. The opposite has proved to be the case. The foundation upon which the Welfare State was built has crumbled.

Existing attitudes and theories at first made it difficult for politicians to recognise that tidal shifts in the economic, social and cultural waters are underway which suggest that the political and welfare system of tomorrow is likely to be very different from the one we have today.

At the same time that some of the forces which impact on everyday life move from national government, become transnational and global so also, because the individual becomes ever more skilled and gains the ability to shape his own life, other forces move down to the level of the street and neighbourhood.

The result is likely to be that the urban areas of this country will themselves assume the status of City States. Birmingham's, Sheffield's and Nottingham's relations with Bristol, Chicago, Delhi and Barcelona are becoming as important as those they have with Whitehall. At the same time, the principle of subsidiarity dictates that as these new Local Authority-wide urban identities grow, others, will shrink as they are undertaken at a local neighbourhood level.

In place of the sectional industrial work place and class-based battles and structures of the twentieth century, there is the prospect of all the political parties having to run fast to catch up with these changing transnational and very local social circumstances, reflect the more sophisticated sentiments and skills of ordinary people and so change the very nature of the political system and the way society is stewarded.

It turns out that the apparently politically irreconcilable self-reliant individual of Conservatism and the collective support of Labour are, in real life, parts of the same whole. When we get the balance right between them we can generate the energy required for the creation of social capital, the mutual bonds and associations through which people live. In place of a society which 'grates' we can create one which 'flows'.

Capacity Builders, civic and economic entrepreneurs have already begun the task of putting back into society many of the essential harmonising features which have been eroded over the course of a century. In doing so in practical, common sense, terms rather than in a political way, they have begun to show us all how to combine the best features of individualism and collectivism and point to a new kind of politics. After a series of very expensive failed attempts at urban renewal over a 30 year period we can see that it is at last possible to include and regenerate excluded neighbourhoods which face multiple problems by reforming the way care is managed in society.

The third way is not a compromise between the extremes of left and right. It aims to include the third force of active citizens in the management of their own lives in the neighbourhoods where they live and raise their families. It is this powerful alliance of citizens, the enabling state and the regulated market that defines the basis of the third way.

The principles behind this way and the reforms it implies can be summarised as follows:

1. We now know that in order to deliver welfare services we do not need to increase taxation, as the collectivist would have us do, nor do we need to lower taxes, as the individualist suggests. Rather, it is important to use existing money in quite different ways. It is vital that the taxpayer is able to see where their money is going – not on unproductive state bureaucracies but to needy individuals and locally managed agencies, which can use that money to good purpose. It is essential that local people gain a sense of ownership over these

independent, taxpayer funded, cost centres so that they become local social assets through which welfare is delivered. Thus, the givers, the administrators and the receivers are connected in a transparent way, can identify with each other and recognise the role which each plays.

2. For most of the last century of the last millennium the Labour Party wanted to nationalise communal or social as well as economic endeavour. But, it only succeeded in stifling it while the right have sought to privatise it and unintentionally ignored all those people who cannot stand on their own feet without mutual support and encouragement. Neither nationalisation nor privatisation can unlock the social or economic potential of excluded people or those who wish to assist them.

3. Self-belief, skills, determination and power cannot be redistributed and given to people who do not have them. Nor, once lost, can they be regained overnight. People have to build these virtues for themselves by associating with each other and constructing a new social hinterland. Replenishing eroded social capital is hard work and takes as much time as greening the desert.

4. It follows that the size and scope of government should neither increase nor diminish. It is the nature of it which should change. It should develop a fresh enabling role, facilitate and not provide. It must develop from being a purely representative democracy in which people can only vote for others to represent them to also being a participatory democracy in which people themselves are directly involved in shaping their own lives every day of the week.

   It has been said that representative democracy is accountable. In the formal sense, it is. But, participatory democracy holds people to account for one another close at home where opinion, criticism and response can have immediate and telling effect. For example, a school is much more accountable if it has to justify the way it spends its budget to parents and local businesses in its own catchment area than when its budget can not be distinguished from those of all other schools. The same is true of the housing estate, health centre, Community Development Trust and neighbourhood.

5. Once participatory democracy and the governance by people of their own neighbourhoods becomes the order of the day, the conventional party politics of left and right becomes largely redundant, especially at the local level. Most people are not concerned with political theory but with more practical matters. Is there litter in my street and, if so, how do I get it moved? Is my child and my neighbour frightened to go out at night and, if so, how can I help them to feel safer? Etc., etc., etc. These are practical, every day, all party and non party questions, which require answers which are not prejudiced by theory or political caucuses.

6. We have to conclude that collectivists have committed their ultimate error in supposing that because the poor do not have power or wealth then they must organise themselves politically and take them from those who do have them. It follows from this assumption that rival parties – one for the poor class and one for the rich – must lock horns in a class war which one might win eventually and the other might lose.

It is increasingly difficult to grasp that anyone can ever have supposed that the route to social progress was via conflict and victory in work between workers and management and in politics between the poor and the rich, the haves and the have-nots. But they did and influential politicians still do. Lord Hattersley was still insisting, even in 1998, that "the call for consensus is wrong" and that to determine issues "on their merit" is "dangerous for socialism." Yet, it is clear to most people that we must play to each other's strengths, not attack each other's weaknesses or accentuate our capacity to distrust and beat each other. Bringing the different sections of a community and the wider society into mutually productive alignment is not a "compromise" but an energising and liberating virtue. Indeed, bringing different interest groups together does more than create a simple sum of them. It gives added value. It creates communal bonds and a mutual understanding which ties people together and generates fresh energy, growth, 'flair' and 'flow.' In helping others rather than vying with them, we help ourselves and multiply rather than redistribute scarce resources.

7. Like the bankrupt mill and mine of the industrial era, so the failing services of the industrially derived Welfare State must be closed down and reopened under new management to suit a new purpose.

This will, we discovered, entail the fundamental reappraisal of the role of the communal or voluntary sector and the need for people to play a responsible and active role in developing and sustaining the quality of social life. Inevitably this will result in the public sector reappraising its function and the blending of participatory with representative democracy.

Too often in the past politicians have supposed that they know best and that ordinary people, especially those in the most difficult areas in the country, can't play any part in their own solution. We now know that this no longer holds true, if it ever did.

Ordinary people know rather more than politicians about what is right for them and their neighbourhoods. With the careful encouragement which a new breed of Capacity Builder and Civic Entrepreneur can give, local people and local businesses hold many of the answers to questions which have bedevilled us for 100 years. It is now clear that the role of local and central government is not to impose solutions but to devise policies which enable more local and non political partnerships to flourish.

The days of Representative democracy's monopolistic service provision are ending. Those of participatory democracy's self-help and mutual assistance are on the ascendant. A quantum leap in the development of democracy is under way at this moment. Where it will eventually lead is difficult to foresee. At the very least, however, it will transform local government. It may well also transform national government and the very nature of our society.

8. Many of the assumptions and political dichotomies of the twentieth century seem destined to fade as a fresh and radical alternative emerges, a third way which entails using neither the public nor the private sectors alone to deliver services. The woefully weakened "third" or "community" sector can, if strengthened, play a vital role – which also changes the black and white way we view the public and private sectors. The community sector can rejuvenate civil society close at home, where most people and certainly children find their identity, well being and purpose in life.

   The advantage is clear. The third sector embodies mutual responsibility, which is rooted in local neighbourhoods. It promotes a powerful sense of personal ownership, generates ethical investment, creates civic assets and local pride. It enhances and develops democracy by adding the quality of personal and communal participation to that of simple representation. It builds the capacity of ordinary people to shape and improve the quality of their lives, almost imperceptibly moving to a situation where the state no longer dominates but enables others in the private and third sectors to provide. It re-introduces tax-givers to the agencies and people they fund. It creates mutual appreciation, inclusion and the harmony of one society.

9. If free people are to live together in harmony and not conflict and support each other in sickness and in health, then once scorned overarching common values and a set of traditions which summarise and teach them become a common sense and practical necessity. Reinventing a culture which through a moral covenant upholds these vital guides to choice and judgement will take time. Greening the a-cultural, overly rational, desert which has been bleaching social ground for so long is a huge undertaking. It will require changes as profound as those introduced by the Enlightenment and is far beyond the scope of any government, party or section of society.

   And, it is unquestionably radical. Despite the investment of billions of pounds, the Welfare State has failed to help the 30% of the population who live in the nation's most troubled areas. Their plight has, if anything, got worse and not better. Those Capacity Builders and Civic Entrepreneurs who have not waited for Welfare Reforms but started the long, slow, process of capacity building and empowerment have shown that they can reach the parts of society which the conventional service delivery could not touch. This discovery, (or is it re-discovery) should be worth its weight in social and political gold.

These developments are progress not privatisation, liberation not competition. They change the very nature of government and entail a new compact or covenant between the people and local and central government.

This covenant is about to be invited onto the centre of the stage by a range of voices calling from the Four Corners of the land. They can be heard in Bromley by Bow, Birkenhead, Toxteth, Easterhouse, and Balsall Heath. For some time, these voices were hesitant and spoke in whispers. Then they became an audible buzz. Today, the sound they make has risen to become a clarion call to unite the nation and propel us through the first decades of the new Millennium.

Can the most senior politicians, clerics and opinion leaders hear this call? Will they act upon it? Will they go with the flow, shift their emphasis to steering while letting others row? Can they respond to, respect and resource the power and emotional intelligence of the people? Will they act as midwife as the Welfare State gives birth to the Welfare Society? Will we witness an Urban Renaissance of the kind designed to grace the early decades of the first century of the third millennium?

Charts & Figures

Bibliography

Ashdown, Paddy	Beyond Westminster	Simon and Schunter
Atkinson, Dick	Radical Alternative, Orthodox Consensus	Heinemann
	Radical Urban Solutions	
	Cities of Pride	
	The Common Sense of Community	DEMOS
	Towards Self-governing Schools	IEA
Bright, Jon	Turning the Tide	DEMOS
Canterbury, Archbishop of	Faith in the City	Church House
Csikszentmihalyi, Mihaly	Living Well	Weidenfeld and Nicolson
Darling, Alastair	The Changing Welfare State	HMSO
Davies, Nick	Dark Heart	Vintage
Elstee, John	Local Justice	Cambridge Press
Etzioni, Amitai	The spirit of community	Crown
Field, Frank	Making Welfare Work	Institute of community studies
Fordham, Scott, Kemp Richard and Crowsley, Paul	Going the extra mile	The JRF
Gidens, Anthony	The Third Way	Polity
Golman, Daniel	Emotional Intelligence	Bloomsbury
Handy, Charles	The Age of Unreason	Hutchinson
Holman, Robert	A new deal for social welfare	Lion
Leadbeater, Charles	The Rise of the Social Entrepreneur	DEMOS
Leadbeater, Charles and Goss, Sue	Civic Entrepreneurship	DEMOS
Leadbeater, Charles	Living on Thin Air	Viking
Osborne and Gaebler	Reinventing Government	Addison Wesley and Renguine
Philips Melanie	All shall have prizes	Little Brown
Power, Anne & Tunstall Rebecca	Dangerous Disorder	The Joseph Rowntree Foundation
	Swimming against the tide	
Power, Anne & Mumford Katherine	The Slow Death of Great Cities	
Power, Anne	Estates on the Edge	Macmillan Press
Rifkin, Jeremy	The End of Work	Tarcher Puntnan

Rodgers, Lord Richard	Towards Urban Renaissance	HMSO
Shumacher, Eric	Small is Beautiful	Penguin
Sacks, Johnathon	The Politics of Hope	Jonathan Cape Sacks,
Sacks, Johnathon	Faith in the Future	Darton, Longman and Treld
Skidelsky Robert	Beyond the Welfare State	Social Market Foundation
Stewart Valarie	The David Solution	Gower
Taylor, Marilyn	Unleashing the potential	The Joseph Rowntree Foundation
Taylor, Marilyn	Top Down meets Bottom Up	The Joseph Rowntree Foundation
Thake, Stephen	Staying the course	
Thake, Stephen	Practical People, Noble Causes	The JRF
Van der Eyben, Williams	Home-Start	Home-Start consultancy
Wadhams, Chris	Thursday's Children	The Quest Trust
Wales, The Prince of	A Vision of Britain	Doubleday
Wann, Mai	Building Social Capital	IPPR
Willetts, David	Civic Conservatism	The Social Market Foundation
Wilson, James, Q	The Moral Sense	Free Press
Willetts, David	Modern Conservatism	Penguin Books
Whelan, Robert	Octavia Hill	IEA
Whelan, Robert	Involuntary Action	IEA